TWELVE-HOUSE TAROT SPREADS

❖

USES AND VARIATIONS

By Elizabeth Hazel

Text, illustrations and graphics by Elizabeth Hazel © 2020

Tarot card images are from *The Whispering Tarot* by Elizabeth Hazel © 2008

ISBN 978-1-7353770-1-8

All rights reserved. No part of this book may be reproduced, stored in or introduced into a retrieval system, or transmitted in any form or by any means (electronic, mechanical, photocopying, recording or otherwise) without the prior written permission of the copyright holder/publisher of this book.

The owner of this book has permission to print the blank spread forms given from pages 79-113 for personal use only. The forms are not to be scanned or digitally transmitted or shared on the internet without written permission from the author.

The scanning, uploading, and distribution of this book via the internet or via any other means without the permission of the publisher is illegal and punishable by law. Please purchase only authorized printed editions and do not participate in or encourage electronic piracy of copyrighted materials.

Your support of the author's rights is greatly appreciated.

KOZMIC KITCHEN PRESS

www.kozmickitchenpress.com

TABLE OF CONTENTS

Introduction

Chapter 1: Construction of the Twelve-House Arrangement   1

Chapter 2: The Twelve Houses   15

Chapter 3: The Cosmic Cross Spread   25

Chapter 4: Variation I: Sequential 12-House Spread   35

Chapter 5: Variation II: Polarity 12-House Spread   41

Chapter 6: Variation III: Spiral 12- House Spread   49

Chapter 7: The Vala Cross   55

Chapter 8: The Expanded Cosmic Axis Spread   61

Chapter 9: The Etteilla 12-House Spread   67

End Matter

Suggested Reading   77

Appendix: Blank Spread Forms   79

About the Author   115

Introduction

Greetings, readers! Welcome to the *Twelve-House Tarot Spreads: Uses and Variations*, and thank you for purchasing this book. Hopefully you'll be entertained, learn interesting things, roll your eyes at my twisted sense of humor, and—best of all—discover an abundant variety of new ways to use the twelve-house spread.

When I started reading adult books as a child, I thought it was hugely unfair that kids got books with pictures but adults did not. It was my first big tip-off that being an adult would not be nearly as good as my sheltered, suburban, ethnically homogenous, religiously straight-jacketed, non-genetically modified but antibiotically-overdosed adolescent paradise.

The good times returned with digital publishing, which offer authors the opportunity of adding copious illustrations to their text. My inner Maurice Sendak celebrated with a wild rumpus! Maddened months went by as I wrote and drew illustrations with Frankensteinian fervor, until finally I could flip the digital switch and scream to the heavens, "It's ALIVE!"

(Roiling clouds in a tormented sky boom with dramatic crash and roll of thunder. Scene fades, segues into a cheesy cartoonish sunrise over placid meadow with flowers and tweeting birds as the text begins...)

Brides obtain "something old, something new, something borrowed and something blue" to wear when they get married. Borrowing is a time-honored occult practice. Well-established techniques from an existing divination method are modified and grafted into a new divination method. The transfer may confer a whiff of respectability. If an old method works, then surely the new method – with its pilfered sprinkles of chocolaty goodness – will work, too.

Astrology was a Hellenic synthesis of star-watching techniques borrowed from conquered Alexandrian territories that included the Mesopotamia and Egypt (circa 330 BCE). It became popular and spread throughout the ancient world. After the fall of Rome, astrology was further developed by brilliant scholars in the Arabic world who invented algebra, calculus and trigonometry to improve their astrological calculations. It was taught at a network of Islamic universities throughout the Middle East, northern Africa and in Spain. Astrology revived in Europe during the Middle Ages as secular education became more accessible. Medicine, mathematics, and astrology were taught side-by-side in Europe until the 1700s.

Copernicus rediscovered that the Sun was the center of the solar system in 1497. [1] He spent the rest of his life working on a book about the heliocentric theory called **De Revolutionibus**. He died with a copy of the first edition in his hands in 1543. Galileo was convicted of heresy for adhering to the heliocentric theory in 1632. Eventually the idea of a sun-centered solar system gained acceptance. Astrology was discredited by rationalist skeptics. If the sun is the center of the solar system, how can earth-centered astrology work? [2] Astrology fell into disrepute but didn't disappear entirely.

The game of Tarocchi crept into the mix and turned into a popular form of divination. Medieval scholar and professor Judith Merkle Riley suggests in **The Oracle Glass** [3] that practitioners, mainly women, were giving tarot readings by the mid-1600s. This is quite probable – both the early date and the fact that it was a form of divination practiced widely by women. Speculation that tarot cards were used for divination long before written evidence appeared isn't unreasonable.

In Riley's scholarly estimation, women (in particular) were eager for accessible sources of prophecy. Fortune-telling was a solid, income-producing trade. Astrology was a male-dominated profession that required literacy and mathematical skills. Tarot-reading wasn't dependent on literacy and tarot cards were an available, affordable product. Early tarot-reading methods were probably passed down through families or even through apprenticeships. But sometimes fortune-telling overlapped with the sale of love potions, charms, abortifacients, and "inheritance powders" (arsenic). Fortune-telling wasn't entirely respectable but it was tolerated. Witchcraft and murder were illegal.

French and Italian mystics were a part of the "underground river" of occultism and the secret societies that swelled toward the French Revolution in the 1790s. British mysticism developed at its own pace with an eclectic mix of continental and original ideas. The last of the "late medieval" astrologers and writers (so-called because they were the last to practice medieval methods) were British.

The rampant development of continental mysticism was driven, in part, by politics. The scope of armed conflicts grew after the Renaissance. Trade, communications, and nautical skills improved, but so did the arts of warfare. The European monarchies of the 1600's and 1700's made life capricious for the general public. There were interminable wars over territorial control and religion. Droughts, famines, and epidemics added to the instability. Monarchs debased currencies to pay war debts and caused heavy inflation. The Reformation sundered the power of the Roman Catholic Church for the first time in centuries. The exclusive dominance of kings, church, and even the earth as the center of the universe was eroding. The vast potential of the New World became an increasingly attractive option for the adventurous and the oppressed.

Uncertain times drive people to seek knowledge of the future in any way they can get it. With the astrological mother-ship temporarily eclipsed, other forms of divination filled the vacuum: palmistry, water scrying, wax readings, and psychometry, to name a few. Tarot divination was accessible and possibly widespread, but the methods remained undocumented until the tarot were co-opted by European mystics and occultists toward the end of the 18th century.

Elements of astrology were borrowed and applied to the tarot in its infancy. The Sun, Moon and Star were included in the trump series from the very beginning. The earliest extant books on divinatory tarot were written by French occultists in the 1780's. Etteilla, the author of one of these early books, did two critically important things that are at the bedrock of subsequent tarot development: he assigned astrological attributions to tarot cards, and he invented the twelve-house spread. A description of Etteilla's method is given in Chapter 9. His contributions reinforced the link between the earthly tarot and the starry heavens.

Endnotes

[1] Claudius Ptolemy, author of **Tetrabiblos** and the **Almagest**, made no mention of the sun-centered system in his books. He may not have thought that it was terribly relevant (see Note 2, below), or simply wasn't aware of it. Expert astrologer and translator James Herschel Holden posited that Ptolemy was an encyclopedist hired to supply a wealthy client with a library rather than a practicing astrologer. Due to the vagaries of early medieval book production, Ptolemy's books enjoyed widespread circulation and became the definitive gospel of European astrology. Ptolemy's earth-centered system was so thoroughly accepted that arguments to the contrary were not only wrong but heretical.

[2] The rationalists who promulgated the new sciences extended the mechanistic Aristotelian worldview. The Platonic and Pythagorean cosmological and metaphysical foundations of astrological practice (which developed circa 300 to 100 BCE) were trampled in the dust. Geocentric or earth-centered astrology was *not* based on the belief that the earth is the center of the solar system. To the contrary, astrology was geocentric *in spite of* the sun-centered system. Aristarchus (circa 300 BCE) wrote that the Sun was the center of the solar system. The Pythagoreans and even the Egyptians were apparently aware of it, too, along with the knowledge that the Earth is round. These things weren't a big secret way-back-when, but they weren't relevant to astrology. Astrological cal-

culations are made from an earth-centered perspective because people live on earth! Charts are calculated for the specific location of an individual's birth. The individual is the "center" upon which the influences of the Moon and planets are imprinted at birth. Continuing planetary movements are always compared to the natal template. The birth chart isn't fate carved in stone, but it does outline certain potentials. As one astrologer said to me, nothing that isn't in the birth chart can happen, but anything that is in the birth chart may happen.

The sun, moon, planets and stars appear to rotate around the earth. This apparent motion is the experiential reality of humanity. These visual "truths" take precedence over the astronomical facts of a sun-centered system. The 20th century mystical scholar Titus Burckhardt (**The Mystical Astrology of Ibn 'Arabi**, Fons Vitae, 2001) argues that experiential truths are far more valuable than astronomical facts, and that these facts can actually be harmful. His argument goes like this: Children are taught that the sun is the center of the planetary system and that the earth is round. What children are being taught is to disregard the truth of their senses and to believe modern humanity is vastly superior to ancient humanity. These teachings also conveniently ignore the proof that ancient people knew the Sun was the center of our system and that the earth is round. I suppose it would be far too controversial to teach children that the facts of the cosmos were known in the ancient world, and that misinformation was promulgated by an oppressive, patriarchal religion until Galileo was brave enough to take a stand against it.

Galileo is a hero of science, but he also precipitated the Mexican divorce between astrology and astronomy. We live in a world that's been complicated by the blurry relationship between truths and facts; and the relative values of each can be used as blunt weapons.

[3] **The Oracle Glass** by Judith Merkle Riley. Reed Business Information Systems, 1994. A fascinating historical novel that describes of fortune-telling franchises and girl apprenticeships during the reign of Louis XIV. The late Judith Merkle Riley's books are little jewels, every one.

Faerie Fetch by E M Hazel 1998

CHAPTER 1

CONSTRUCTION OF THE TWELVE-HOUSE CHART FORM

The art of chart-drawing has changed and developed over twenty-three centuries. The 12-house form borrowed by tarotists is a testament to humanity's perpetual fascination with the stars, and the ever-present desire to gain personal meaning and forecasts from movements in the sky. When you use the 12-house spread, imagine the sands of ancient Egypt and Babylon beneath your feet.

An astrological chart attempts to show the earth-bound individual's relationship with the solar system and outer space. This is a big job for a piece of paper! Chart-rendering involves many compromises that squash the dimensions of space into a flat graphic representation. It isn't perfect, but it gets the job done.

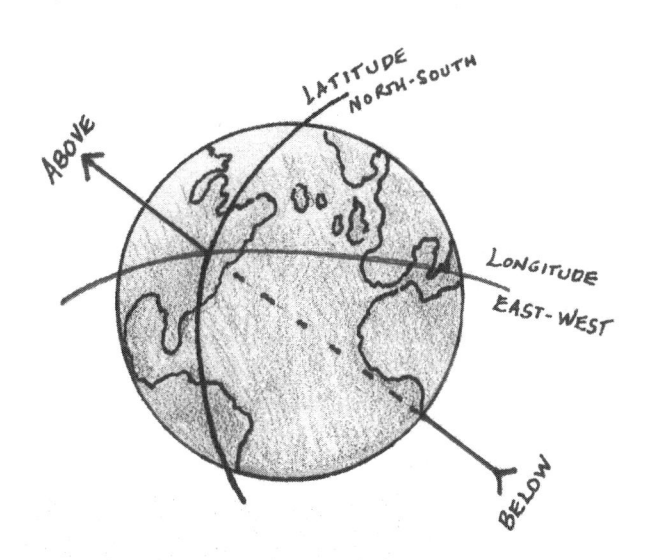

A flat chart, drawn or printed onto a piece of paper, creates invisible but very real liabilities for inexperienced astrologers. It tests the visualization capacity of experienced astrologers who have (more or less) learned how to mentally inflate the thing into a three-dimensional representation of our solar system against the backdrop of the stars orbiting in the fourth dimension, time. This is why intensely dedicated astrologers can seem unhinged from the present. People who spend decades tracking the locations of orbiting planets in relation to one another and to the stars are prone to some side-effects.

A flat 12-house arrangement doesn't present these problems to the tarot reader. Like any tarot spread, the 12-house spread is simply an organized arrangement of cards on the table. Cards are flat, the table's surface is flat, and so the flat chart form fits right into the dog-and-pony show.

In this chapter, I'll discuss the astronomical considerations that influenced how ancient astrologers drew star charts. Esoteric meanings were entwined with the elements of chart construction.

THE CIRCLE

A circle is an esoteric symbol of the whole. A circle doesn't have a top or bottom, a beginning or an end. The Sun and Moon appear to be circular in shape. Both are associated with cycles of life and growth. The seasons seem to rotate in an endless pattern called the circle of life. A person comes "full circle" when returning to a situation from the past. Pagans cast a sacred circle when they begin their rituals to contain sacred space. Besides containment, circles are an expression of inclusion and exclusion. A person can belong to a circle of friends or be excluded from it. Theater-in-the-round and the big ring of a circus allow the audience to see everything.

The Pythagoreans believed that the circle was the perfect geometric shape. With the emphasis on circles on earth, it's little wonder that humans started to project invisible circles into the sky. The twelve constellations of the zodiac are contained, for the most part, within the *ecliptic*, a wide, circular band of the sky. The celestial equator is the midpoint - 0° of the ecliptic. In a solar year, the Sun shifts from north to south and back again. The other planets stay pretty much within the ecliptic, but occasionally stray a few degrees outside of the northern and southern boundaries (look at me, mom, no hands!).

There are plenty of other constellations in, above, and below the ecliptic. The ancient peoples of Mesopotamia selected constellations within the ecliptic that they associated with the seasonal time-keeping of the Sun. Identifiable constellations made it easier to track planetary movements. This is the origin of the twelve signs of the zodiac. Projecting imaginary circles onto the sky helps people track the movements of celestial bodies.

A circle suggests the idea of rotation. As the earth spins on its tilted axis, the constellations appear to roll upward from the eastern horizon. If you watch the sky at night, the view changes a little in an hour and quite a bit over three or four hours. If you watch the sky all night, about half of the zodiac will pass through the sky. The zodiac and other constellations provide a steady, stable backdrop that rotates at a constant speed, while the Moon and planets appear to zig and zag in front of the stars at varying rates of speed.

Circles can describe a circumference like the earth's equator. The circles of longitude and latitude on a globe or map are drawn in relation to the equator. Circles also describe boundaries, like the Tropics of Cancer and Capricorn, which are the bounds of the ecliptic projected onto earth's surface.

In outer space, there's a celestial equator, a galactic equator, and a supergalactic equator. Since the earth orbits with a tilted axis, seasonal intersections with these cosmic equators coincide with the solstices and equinoxes.

The twelve astrological houses are contained within a circle.[1] This allows an astrologer to draw the location of the planets within the circle of the zodiac. A chart form is always drawn the same way; only its contents will differ. An astrological chart is an image of the cosmic clock frozen at a particular moment in time.

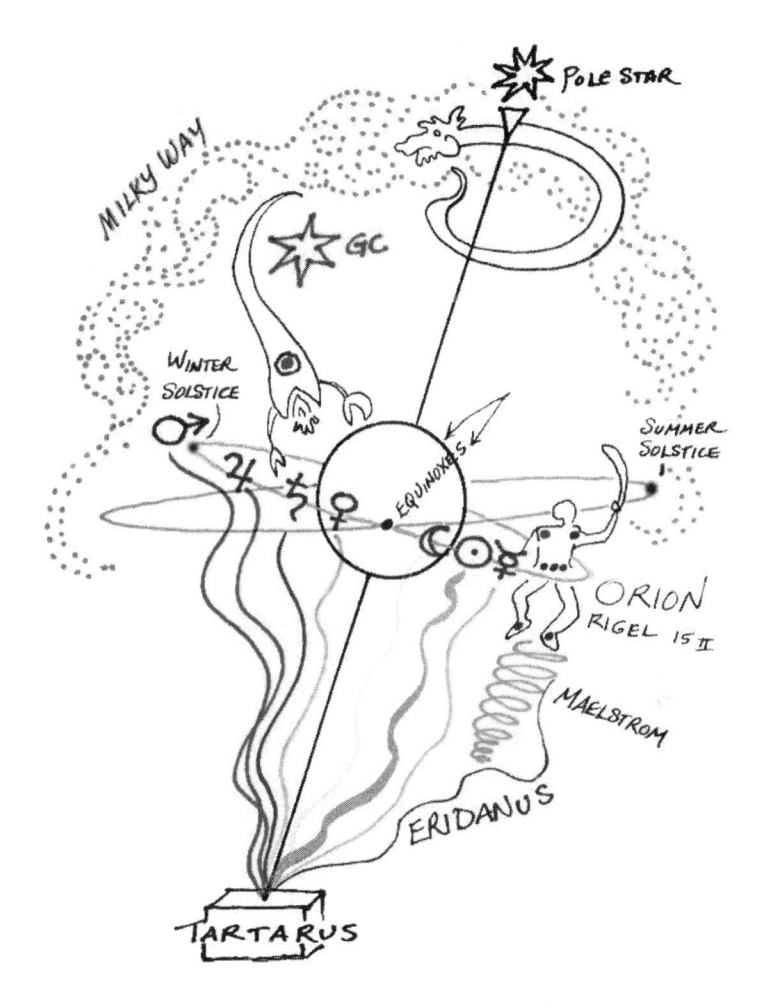

The ancient cosmos. Planets orbit around the earth inside a sphere of stars. The celestial and galactic equators intersect at the equinoxes. The Scorpion's Tail curls around the Galactic Center (GC). The seven rivers of Tartarus, the underworld, flow upward from the Cube of Saturn, and become rivers of light, the paths of the seven visible planets. Orion stands near the point of Summer Solstice with his left foot (Rigel) in another celestial river, the constellation Eridanus.

Think of the planets as actors or gods. The zodiac is the set or backdrop on the stage, or the dwelling places of the gods, who have their favorite and least-favorite places. Placing the planets and signs into a chart form with twelve houses helps an astrologer figure out what the actors are doing: what they're talking about, how they're getting along, and the plot line of the drama they're enacting.

The circle is an enduring symbol of the whole. Circles and spheres are the primary geometrical shapes used to describe the location of the contents of the cosmos. In the astrological 12-house form, the individual is the fixed point around which the circle and its celestial contents are drawn.

THE HORIZON

The horizon divides the circle in half. In the 12-house form this is called the **Ascendant-Descendant axis**. (ASC/DSC) The Ascendant is east, where the Sun, stars and planets rise, become visible and share light, and confer life. The Descendant is west, where celestial bodies set and disappear as they sink into the underworld.

Splitting the circle creates two hemispheres. The upper half of the circle is the outer world. It's what is visible, what's above ground, what's externalized and manifest. In an astrological chart, the upper hemisphere is the individual's external public life. It's where the person encounters reality, other people, and the world. People take and learn things from the upper realm to process in the lower realm, or create things in the lower realm to share with the upper realm.

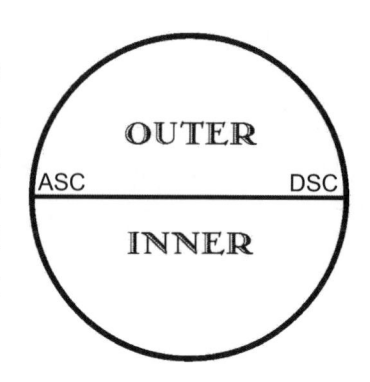

The bottom half of the circle beneath the horizon is the inner world. Things here are shadowy, invisible, or hidden. It's a private place. What's contained here may not be entirely visible to the upper world. The lower hemisphere is the interior life of the individual. Things that develop here may remain hidden, or be taken or projected into the upper hemisphere.

The horizon is critical because it delineates the inner and outer, but it's a permeable barrier. And the Ascendant-Descendant axis is a two-way street. The individual can encounter someone coming from the other direction. It is the **axis of encounters**.

To keep it simple, the upper hemisphere is called "Outer," the lower hemisphere is called "Inner."

THE MIDHEAVEN

A vertical axis divides the circle into two hemispheres that may be called right and left, or east and west. The arrow at the top of this line is the Midheaven or *Midi Coeli* (Upper Heaven) which is abbreviated as "MC." The opposite end or bottom is called the Nadir, the *Imum Coeli* (Lower Heaven), which is abbreviated as "IC." The **MC-IC axis** is the axis of experience; or of origins and destinations.

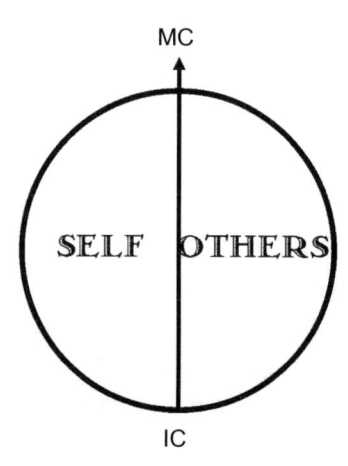

The Midheaven points south/up and the Nadir points north/down. This a side-effect of the compromises made to depict three dimensions on a piece of paper. The left or eastern hemisphere, which contains the Ascendant, belongs to the individual. This is the area where the individual gains life. The soul manifests into a body, gets a name, has self-identity and self-interests. You are a soul, you have a body.

The right or western hemisphere contains the Descendent, which signifies others: other people, partners, opposites, adversaries, and things that enhance, challenge, and deplete life. The MC-IC axis is as permeable as the Ascendant-Descendant axis. Things are exchanged from side to side between the individual and others. Again, a division but not a barrier.

THE COSMIC CROSS

The two axes intersect and form the Cosmic Cross. The cross is a symbol of manifestation: the spirit descends and takes material form. In an astrological chart, the Cosmic Cross shows the orientation of the individual who gains life at a fixed point in time and space. The Cosmic Cross helps to map out the individual's potentials for manifestation in the world.

The map is not the terrain! The birth chart is a template for manifestation. Each person has unique sets of pre-existing circumstances at birth. These are followed by a unique series of encounters (ASC-DSC axis) that produce experiences (MC-IC axis) that mold the person in time and space. People grow, mature, and change in time, and may occupy many locations in a city, region, or around the globe. The birth chart is a map of the starting point, a seed with manifold potentials. In addition to providing a fixed point of orientation, the Cosmic Cross is the armature providing structure for the contents of the circle: zodiac signs and fixed stars, planets, asteroids, and sensitive points that are derived from these (like the Part of Fortune).

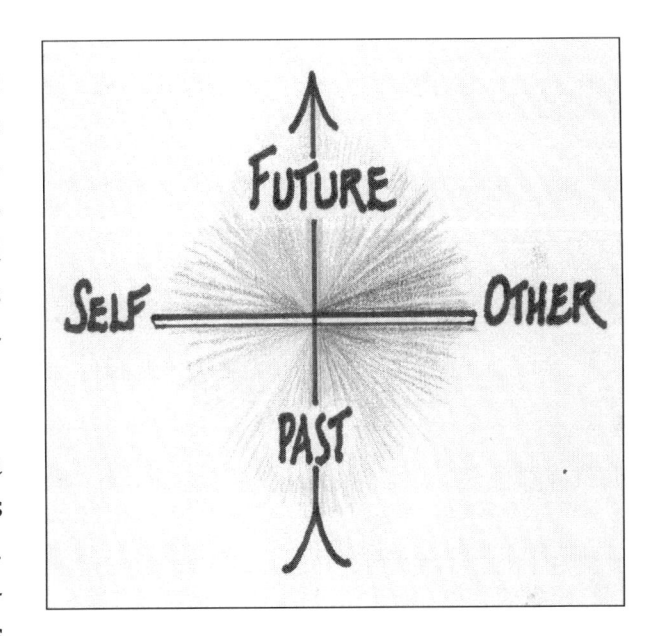

The cross divides the circle into four quadrants. These are all-important quadrants in astrology, and they're equally important for interpreting a 12-house spread.

The first quadrant belongs to the **Inner-Self**, and contains houses 1 – 2 – 3. This quadrant is completely personal and centers on the individual's body, mind, skills, motivations, and movements. In the battle of nature vs. nurture, the first quadrant represents nature, the traits and attributes inherent to the individual.

The second quadrant belongs to **Inner-Others** and contains houses 4 – 5 – 6. This quadrant isn't completely personal, but is still fairly private and somewhat shielded from the outer world. It shows the family of origin and ancestors, the home and domestic environment, love relationships, creative efforts, progeny, and the health or illness of his/her body. This quadrant represents the nurturing portion of nature vs. nurture, the qualities imprinted on the individual through association with family.

The third quadrant belongs to **Outer-Others** and contains houses 7 – 8 – 9. This quadrant is above the horizon. Its contents are open and visible. This is where the individual encounters other people (not limited to family members), enters and exits relationships, exchanges of money and knowledge, engages in long-term planning, and gains an education that may give him or her a more sophisticated view of the outer world. He or she may partake of the collective curiosity about the divine through spirituality, religion, and philosophy. The first quadrant gives and takes, and the third quadrant takes and gives. Ideally the give-and-take is balanced and flows in both directions. The nature of the individual, conditioned by his/her origins, grows and is further molded by encounters with the outside world.

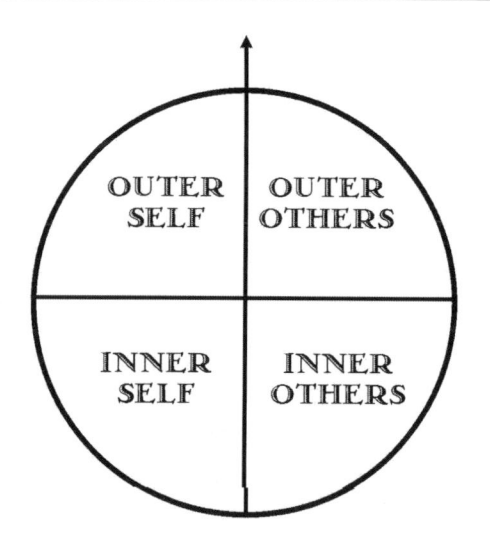

The fourth quadrant belongs to the **Outer-Self** and contains houses 10 – 11 – 12. This is where the individual interacts with the outer world on a wider level through groups, work setting, government and bureaucracies, networks, and associations. This is the realm of labels, titles, designations, and memberships. It's where the "three degrees of separation" phenomenon occurs. The sum of efforts of the previous three quadrants enter the world in the fourth quadrant and succeed or fail. The creative efforts of the second quadrant are judged, accepted or rejected in the fourth quadrant. The fourth quadrant is the quadrant of results, good or bad, private and public.

THE FOUR AXIS POINTS

The four axis points of a chart are called "**pivots**." It means exactly what it sounds like: these are pivotal zones of the chart, where the most important things occur. Each axis point has unique meaning.

The Cosmic Cross formed by the four axis points is both cosmic and personal. It's a symbolic link between the macrocosm and the microcosm. The Earth's pivots are the equinoxes and solstices. Winter solstice is the Earth's Ascendant, the point of beginning and inception; the autumnal equinox is Earth's Midheaven, the point of results and harvests. The planets and stars are a cosmic clock; the zodiac signs mark the hours and the planets are the "hands" of the clock whose intersections coincide with Earth's development and evolution. That's the macrocosm. Individuals are a miniature, microcosmic version of the Earth in relation to the cosmos. The birth chart delineates the individual's personal Cosmic Cross. The zodiac marks the "places" of life while the orbiting planets mark the times when events unfold.

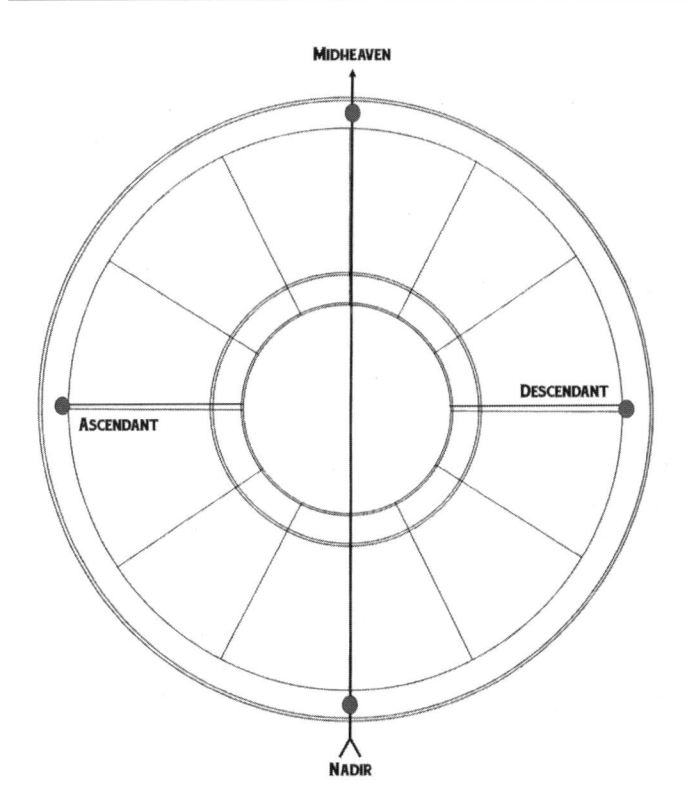

As above, so below.

THE ASCENDANT

The Ascendant or "rising" is exactly what it seems to be – the place in the east where the Sun rises in the morning. The horizon is where the sky meets the earth. Even if you weren't born at sunrise, there's still an eastern and western horizon on the landscape. The Sun always rises in the east and sets in the west. The Ascendant axis corresponds to this natural phenomenon.

The Sun is the animating principle of life and the soul. The Ascendant is the point where the soul joins the body at birth; not sunrise, but soulrise. Energy and anima (spirit) are conferred at this axis point. It is the point where life/body and soul unite to become a newborn human at a particular place and time.

Ancient astrologers attributed the physical body and head to this axis. The Ascendant was the "ship of life," the vessel that contains the soul. It describes the condition of that vessel but not necessarily any mental contents. Modern astrologers have co-opted a great deal of psychology, so now the Ascendant and 1st house correspond to stuff that's in the head, the mind, the psyche, and identity. The Ascendant is considered the "face one shows the world," the primary mask or persona, as well as the face itself.

Tarot Tip: A card that occupies the Ascendant (and by extension, the first house) relates specifically to the individual. It describes his or her personal condition, emotions, and health. The things that appear in the card already exist (pre-existing conditions), so this may card show events leading up to the point where the person sat down to get a tarot reading. It may not show a complete picture of the client's past, but rather the portion of it most relevant to the reading.

THE DESCENDANT

This is the opposite end of the Ascendant axis. If the Ascendant is life, then the Descendant is death. It isn't generally expressed in such a dramatic way, but it wouldn't be incorrect to say that if the Ascendant is soul-rise, then the Descendant is soul-set.

The Descendant provides the seventh house cusp in most house systems, so it has become associated with intimate relationships and one-on-one encounters with other individuals. The Ascendant is Me, the Descendant is You. The Self recognizes the existence of other Selves and learns how to cope, cooperate, and even find joy with them. But not always. Sometimes other people suck. So the Descendant can be the spouse or long-time intimate partner, but it can also be one's adversary. The Descendant is a point of union with the other, but it can also function as a point of contention. Legal and political opponents can occupy this place.

If Clark Kent/Superman is represented by the Ascendant, then both Lex Luthor and Lois Lane occupy the Descendant. The Descendant can love and loathe. Strange, huh? The Descendant is a pivot and pivots include extremes. Since the Descendant represents sunset, it is a place where the individual's powers are diffused and weakened. The Self has to yield space and power to others, share and cooperate.

The Ascendant-Descendant axis has the magnetic powers of attraction and repulsion. As people enter the world at large, they meet and get to know other individuals at varying levels of intimacy. The individual may become acquainted with many people but develops closeness and intimacy with only a very few. The Ascendant-Descendant axis exerts a kind of selective power that narrows the wide spectrum of acquaintances down to a few that receive intense focus from the individual. Relationship karma operates along this axis.

Ancient astrologers viewed the Descendant as a more dangerous place than modern astrologers. Life was fragile; just about anything could go wrong and snuff out life. In addition, marriages were arranged by families. So the marital partner wasn't necessarily a beloved ally who shared life's vicissitudes. The spouse could be a prize or a rotten pickle. There isn't always much choice about who turns into an enemy. Enemies show up like warts, unwelcome and hard to get rid of. A person who is a beloved ally can turn into an adversary, too. This is a tricky pivot!

Modern astrologers attribute a lot more free-will and lovey-dovey-kiss-kiss to the Descendant than ancient astrologers, and are a lot less willing to acknowledge that this is a place where pushing, shoving and fighting can occur. The jury's still out on whether the ancients or moderns are more correct. For individuals who are not married, not in long-term committed relationships, and not in any free-for-all adversarial competitions, this axis extends its meaning to include close personal relationships of almost any type: close friends, friendly long-term co-workers, bosses, and other people that the client frequently interacts with.

Tarot Tip: A card that occupies the Descendant (or by extension the seventh house) refers to close, personal contacts with other individuals. It shows the effect other people have on the client, and whether these people help, harm or hinder the client. This card can show a person (or persons) the client is intensely focused on because of current events or conditions around that person. Look for the clues in the card's imagery as to whether interactions are friendly, intimate, confusing, or hostile.

If more than one person is depicted on the card, the card's meanings may apply to more than one person. Two's can indicate more than one person, as can cards attributed to double signs (Gemini, Virgo, Sagittarius, and Pisces). Knights can be individuals, but also groups with a focal interest. For instance, the Knight of Wands can be a group of salesmen who are always on the move, hastily entering and exiting a building, and always in competition with one another. It could simultaneously be an individual who has hit-and-run encounters with the client. Consider neighboring cards in the 6th and 8th house positions for details about the person or persons shown in the 7th house position.

THE NADIR

This axis represents the roots that sink beneath the ground. It represents ancestors, the family of origin, and the parents (whether biological or adoptive). Ancient astrologers assign the 4th house to the father, whereas modern astrologers sometimes attribute it to the mother, or give the definitely indefinite suggestion that this point represents the less-dominant parent.

The Midheaven points to what's above; the Nadir travels down through the center of the earth and extends into the underworld. It represents physical, ancestral, and esoteric foundations at the root of one's being. It can connect to skeletons, graveyards and ghosts. In fact, the Nadir and fourth house are associated with burial grounds and where the individual's body is placed after death.

The Nadir is all about the past: the karma accumulated from past lives, family and collective karma, and (more or less) the stuff the soul doesn't get to choose before incarnating. These are pre-existing conditions that may include a family's social status and geographic location. Have you ever heard the saying that the reason family members can push your buttons is because they installed them? That's the Nadir. The IC is the root of all those charming life lessons.

The MC-IC axis is associated with *Ananke*, a Greek goddess whose name means *necessity*. A lot of ancient philosophical ideas about the nature of existence were grafted into early cosmological models. The song of life goes something like this: people stumble across their **fate** by being born into a certain society, meeting particular people in it, and interacting with the world. They grapple with the haphazard influences of **fortune** by being at the right or wrong place at the right or wrong time. **Ananke or Necessity** is what the individual has to do to survive the influences of fate and fortune. Then **free will** gets it's big chance! How the individual responds to fate and fortune determines his **destination or destiny**. This is where the IC pivot gets tricky. The IC is the point where all that came before—the family patterns, genetic codes, past karma, conditioned ways of thinking about the world, and past personal experiences—present a challenge to the Ascendant, the individual's unique existence. A person can follow the patterns of the past or break free and make entirely new choices in the present that can shift outcomes in future. Free will is always involved in quandaries about safety or risk.

It isn't all gloom and doom at the bottom. The Nadir represents the origin and early family life. As the person gets older, the 4th house represents the individual's personal domestic situation. On a psychological level, it's the inner depths, the hidden fountain of strength, courage, and resourcefulness, an invisible well that never runs dry. In a Jungian sense, the furthermost depths of the IC link the individual to the collective unconscious. An artist who plumbs these depths may bring forth images and sculptures that ring a universal chord of the collective. The past is the origin of all the seeds that can become the future.

Tarot Tip: The card that occupies the Nadir (and by extension the fourth house) shows what's at the root of the matter, the basis of the situation, endings and beginnings, and incidents in the past that cast light and shadows on the present, and possibly into the future. It can describe the family and domestic situation, the parents and grandparents, and changes of residence. It can show a specific family member of concern to the client. If the 7th house card shows other people the client is concerned with, like good friends, sometimes the spouse appears in the 4th house.

The card may also show the client's relationship with his dwelling space. It may show that the dwelling place is temporary, being renovated, or being changed by people moving in or out. It may show that the client isn't at home very much, or is stuck at home, or that lots of people will be coming in and out of the dwelling.

A Major Arcana card in this position delivers a wealth of meanings. It could indicate another person with the nature of that MA card, or qualities within the individual that are being brought to the forefront through circumstances rooted in past choices and circumstances. It may show outer-world events that impact the domestic situation. There may be past karmic influences churning in the client's present situation. A Major Arcana card can contain all of these types of meanings simultaneously. Its significations have a crucial bearing on the meanings of the card in the Midheaven or 10th house position as its influences rise up through the MC-IC axis. Whether its a Major Arcana or suit card, it's important to get a grip on the meaning of this card.

THE MIDHEAVEN

The Nadir describes the past, roots and origins; the Midheaven points to the future, life-path choices, and the fulfillment of ambitions. Everything at the Nadir is extremely personal, whereas what happens at the Midheaven occurs and manifests in the real world. Results are visible, whether to the client or to the world.

The Midheaven shoots into the sky like an eagle, ready to discover what's out there, what's possible, and what can be achieved. Consequently, the Midheaven can be speculative. Fate, fortune, providence, and free will combine in various measures and encounter Ananke-Necessity to produce destination and destiny. People are always in a process of self-creation. Outcomes aren't static but rather cumulative. If the Ascendant is who you are, the Midheaven is what you're doing with your potential, the personal process-of-becoming that's revealed in the world.

Ancient astrologers didn't think much of free will, although social status could and did change in ancient times. The possibility of status change is a prime topic in ancient astrology texts; writers included descriptions of potential astrological indications that a person would move up the ladder. That included the sign on the Midheaven and the condition of the planet that ruled the Midheaven. Modern society offers more choices to the individual (or we like to pretend it does because it fulfills our idea of how modern civilization should be).

The Midheaven doesn't operate independently from the Nadir. The past and future are always roped together. People repeat their parent's mistakes. People may repeat ancestral patterns without ever realizing it. The nature of family patterns is to repeat. Sometimes breaks occur naturally. Children grow up and move away from home. People die or move away from the individual's location. When it comes to tenacious problems like family dysfunctions, it takes strong motivation and great determination to break the chain.

And of course, breaking through a tenacious family pattern may be a destined act. Ernest Hemingway's mother dressed and treated him as a girl for the first seven years of his life. Hemingway made a hasty escape from his family by volunteering to be an ambulance driver in World War I. For the rest of his life, he exercised enormous determination to prove himself as macho and testosterone-driven as possible through adventures, hunting, and travel to dangerous and exciting places. Those experiences increased his ambition to write. It wasn't a clean escape from his roots, however, since his efforts were fueled with enormous amounts of booze and his relationships with women were full of pitfalls. Two generations later, his granddaughter Muriel embraced a healthy vegetarian lifestyle to break away from her grandfather's cruelty to animals and alcoholism.

Perhaps the pattern of the Hemingway clan is to break family patterns in a manner that's publicly visible and inspires others to emulate them. Behavior that's acceptable in one generation can be intolerable to subsequent generations. The past can be like a grease spot on a shirt; a person may have to live with it, but doesn't have to be defined or limited by it. This can go in the other direction, too. Subsequent generations may build upon what's been accomplished by their forebears or predecessors. Individuals are free to decide which patterns they embrace or abandon.

Making choices and acting on choices is a function of the Midheaven. The term "*life choices*" offers a much wider scope of meaning than "career" in reference to the Midheaven and tenth house. Some people may not give a hoot about having a career. Perhaps marriage and children are the top priority. Perhaps embracing spirituality is the goal. Life choice, not career choice.

Tarot Tip: A card that occupies the Midheaven shows outcomes and results. It may show the direction an individual's life or career can take. It can show things the individual meets in the outer world: bosses and officials, various worldly establishments, the government, rules and regulations, opportunities, choices, limitations an obstacles. It can show opportunities and obstacles to moving forward in life on any level. This card may show possible choices or the result of choices and the conditions that surround it.

The card may show future prospects in *any* avenue of life, like family concerns, marriage and divorce, job and career changes, promotions or job loss, moving and location changes, getting a pet, changing religious affiliations, educational efforts, starting a business, or going into politics. It could show important events that are unfolding within a stable career or lifestyle, or a particular individual who is making a big impact. This card can also show unexpected events or situations that have nothing to do with the topics shown in the previous pivots and house positions. It may be a card about choices that affect the life path and lead to profound adjustments, or the lack of choices. It can show the relative success or failure of one's endeavors.

It's up to the reader to gauge how momentous the card in this position is to the client. There could be important life path changes coming up, or the card could show the client is stuck and unable to effect desired changes. The card could show results or outcomes that take place in a logical progression from current efforts, or something coming from out of the blue. This is the position of results, but also a position of possibilities. It can offer a glimpse of known realities in the world along with speculative possibilities, since this position contains elements of the present *and* future.

CHAPTER 1 REVIEW

- The 12-house form is a legacy of ancient astrology.

- The 12-house spread begins with a circle. Things revolve around a circle.

- The circle is divided in half by the Ascendant-Descendant Axis. Upper-Lower = Outer-Inner.

- The circle is divided again by the Midheaven-Nadir (MC-IC) Axis. Left-Right = Self-Others.

- The two axes form four quadrants. Each quadrant has a unique meaning.

- All four Axis Points are pivotal and have unique meanings. Any card that occupies a pivot is important.

"Aries and Scorpio"

CHAPTER 2

THE TWELVE HOUSES

The twelve houses are formed by dividing each quadrant into three sections. [3 houses x 4 quadrants = 12 houses]. The houses are arranged around the circle, starting with the Ascendant/First House and moving counter-clockwise, to the right, around the circle. The houses are **sequential**: the first house is followed by the second house, the second house is followed by the third house, etc.

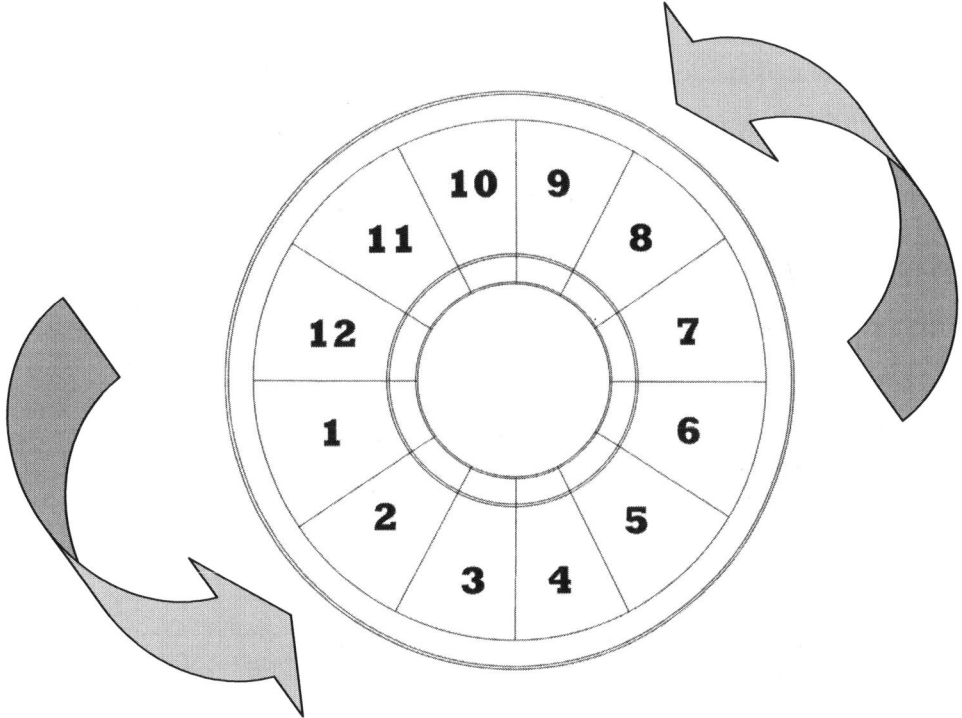

There are other types of relationships implicit between the houses. A primary relationship is **polarity**. A house's meaning relates to the opposite house. The polarities connect even- and odd-numbered houses.

HOUSE POLARITIES

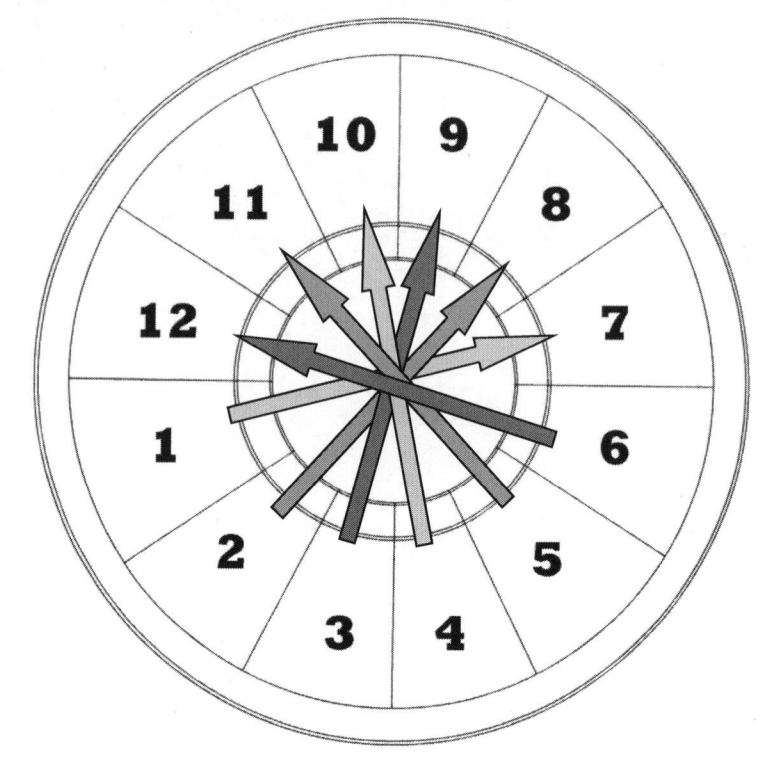

1st house ↔ 7th house

2nd house ↔ 8th house

3rd house ↔ 9th house

4th house ↔ 10th house

5th house ↔ 11th house

6th house ↔ 12th house

Houses also have qualities known as **quadruplicities** and/or **modalities**. Zodiac sign modalities are called cardinal, fixed and mutable. House modalities are *angular, suceedent, and cadent*. These terms are similar but not identical.

Houses 1 – 4 – 7 – 10 are angular and pivotal because they contain (or begin at) the four axis points. These are the most important houses in a 12-house tarot reading. The significations of the cards in these houses manifest most strongly. Angular placements are dynamic and vigorous. Things are actively happening in these houses, or will happen. Relating to others is in progress in houses 1 and 7; turning points, possibilities, internal and external developments are bubbling away in houses 4 and 10. The significations of the four axis points are fully explored later in this chapter.

Houses 2 – 5 – 8 – 11 are suceedent. Suceedent houses succeed or follow the angular houses. The action taking place in the angular houses is succeeded by development in the suceedent houses. They're not quite as powerful as angular houses, but are more stable. These areas of life are longer lasting, but also more difficult to change. A person's 2nd house skills, once acquired, are fairly permanent, as are the 8th house exchanges. Possessions and income sources are likely to be stable unless a card shows otherwise. Relationships in the 5th house sphere, with friends, lovers, and children, can be long-lasting and possibly permanent. The contents of the 11th house depend on the significations of the other houses: if a person practices law as a 2nd house skill and income source, then acquaintances with other attorneys and membership in a bar association will be a part, but not all, of the 11th house. It's also a house of outcomes and results of the 10th house, so can include future developments. Since these are the "love and money" houses, difficult cards placed in them may signify tenacious, long-term problems.

Houses 3 – 6 – 9 – 12 are cadent houses. These are the weakest houses and not especially favorable; indeed, the 6th and 12th houses have nasty reputations. The significations may be invisible, ephemeral, or speculative. The client has more control over what appears in the 3rd and 9th houses, but less control over what shows up in the 6th or 12th houses. The cards that appear here can help or hinder the client. Some of the significations of the cadent houses are changeable and transitory. Health can change (6th), the daily schedule can change (3rd), one's knowledge and understanding can change (9th). Health problems can be chronic, long-term coworkers can be a pain in the butt, a schedule can be overloaded with obligations or excessive commuting, and new information can get the client's panties in a twist. The 12th house is tricky and elusive. Cards here can signify family worries, losses, and hidden concerns, but it can also reveal messages and possibly benefits from remote sources. It may show a focus on spirituality or a hidden love affair. I call the 12th house "the New Jersey of the zodiac." It's the house of left-overs, the things that don't belong anywhere else. Angels, demons, and skeletons in the closets can turn up here, too.

The cards in cadent houses show circumstances that leak onto cards in the angular houses. Things in the 12th house leak into the 1st house; things in the 6th house leak into the 7th house, etc. The 12th house shows the client's hidden matters, while the 6th shows the partner's hidden matters. Consider the cards here in two ways: they relate the contents of the house's meaning, but also can reveal considerations that are spilling into the cards in the angular houses.

MODAL HOUSE RELATIONSHIPS

The quadruplicities or modalities generate specific relationships between houses – a polarity, square, or quadrature. Polarities attract and repel, and allow exchanges and mergers. Squares signify conflicts and challenges. Quadruplicities are dynamic. They stir up motivation and encourage initiative. The person is challenged to fight or flee. The three quadruplicities form three crosses inside of the circle. These crosses all feature one of the four elements on each pole – fire, water, air, and earth. The three zodiacal modalities, cardinal, fixed, and mutable, apply to the elements rather than the zodiac signs. For instance, Gemini is an air sign, and the mode of the air associated with Gemini is mutable. To put it in another way, it is the elements that are cardinal, fixed and mutable; the zodiac signs get modalities by their association with the elements.

HOUSE MODALITIES

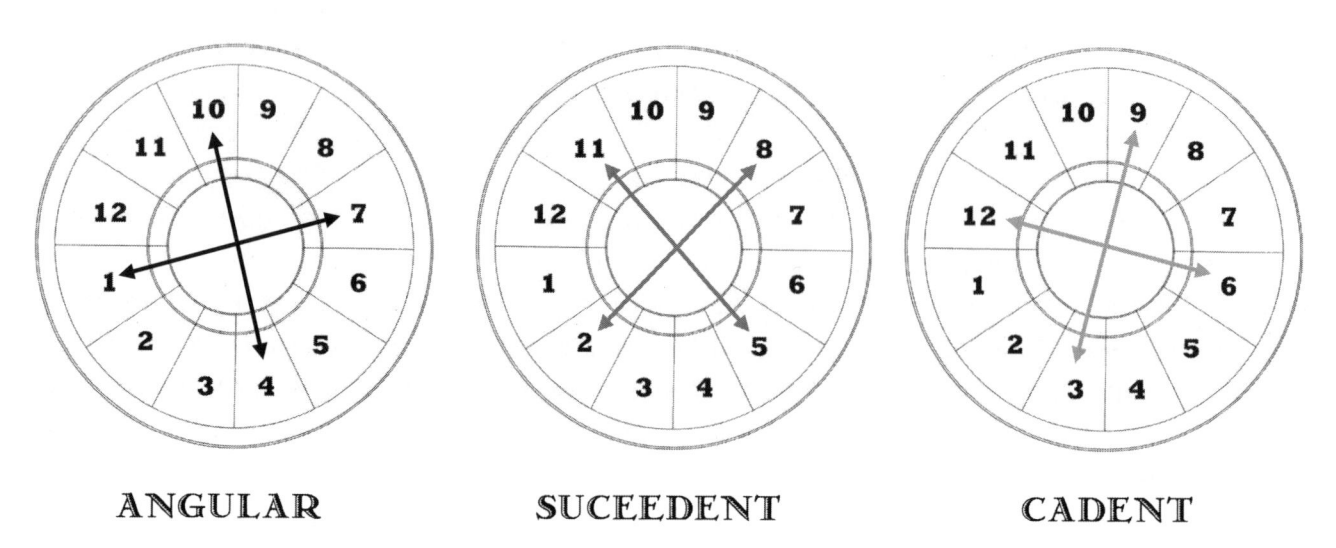

ANGULAR SUCEEDENT CADENT

HOUSE MEANINGS

Ancient and modern views of the houses aren't identical. Technology and psychology were inserted into astrological house systems during the 20th century for better or worse. Some astrologers are attempting to pry the psychological contents out of the houses and restore them to their original condition. Tarotists don't have to get drawn into the battle over ancient and modern house definitions, but they should be aware that house meanings aren't etched in stone. House meanings, like card meanings, have evolved over time.

Tarot cards have well-established divinatory meanings. A beginning tarot student will probably learn that the Two of Wands means "considering possibilities." Well, that's true enough. But the Two of Wands can mean a hundred other things. A core divinatory meaning is like an anchor; it keeps the boat from floating away, but the boat can float some distance in any direction. New and unexpected meanings can turn up at any time – especially when card meanings are merged. Card descriptions offer a range of what a card *might* signify but can't definitively indicate what a card *will* mean in a reading. Divinatory meanings are squiggly little buggers!

House meanings are similarly definitely indefinite. There are core meanings laden with imputed meanings added over the centuries. Houses are **not** zodiac signs or planets. The first house is **not** Aries and **not** Mars. Do not conflate houses with zodiac signs – it's a sloppy habit and leads to a lot of conceptual errors and bad predictions. Conflating houses and signs was a teaching technique from the 20th century that took on a life of its own like an infestation of bed bugs. Please don't go there.

I'll reiterate the theatrical analogy: the planets are the *actors*, the zodiac signs are the *sets and locations*, and the houses are the *scripts* that outline the actor's roles, motivations, and dialogs. Houses show what the planet-actors are talking about or doing in the location/set specified by the zodiac sign. In a 12-house spread, the houses perform the same function. They provide a context of dialog or action for a card. Let's say the Queen of Cups appears in the 3rd house. Her house-related action/dialog will be focused on day-to-day activities, and she occupies the role of a sister or sisterly person. Her zodiacal set is Cancerian and watery, so focused on property, family matters, security, and emotions. She occupies a leaky cadent house so may influence what's going on in the 4th house. The planets and zodiac signs move; the houses stay the same. Any card that lands in a particular house has to pick up the script provided by that house and perform the roles assigned by that house.

A list of house meanings is given below. Stripping complex house meanings down to sound-bites and key words *(gak!)* is a thankless task. There's no way to satisfy all comers or do justice to the houses. People have written entire books on the subject of house meanings. I've added a few meanings from Vedic (Hindu) and ancient astrology that have proven relevant over the years. For those who want to examine house meanings in more depth, there's a list of books for supplemental reading at the end of this book.

First House: The self, the body, the identity; the condition of the self and body

Second House: personal possessions, talents, skills, the pace of work; nourishment (Vedic); self-value, core personal values, what a person is willing to work for

Third House: daily movements, schedules, short messages, siblings; devices for communication and transportation

Fourth House: family, origins, ancestors, domestic conditions, hidden emotional resources, the father, family legacies, especially property, inherited traits

Fifth House: children, love relationships, sexual affairs, friendships, play, creativity, self-expression, gambling, messengers; expectations (whether idealistic or realistic)

Sixth House: work, labor, health and illness, servants and co-workers, aunts and uncles, difficult long-term remediation processes for self and others

Seventh House: partners and spouses, one-on-one relationships, adversaries, battles and lawsuits

Eighth House: inheritance, death, spouse's (or adversary's) money and resources, family transitions; trust given or withheld from others

Ninth House: distant journeys, higher education, religion, spirituality and philosophy, divination, relationship with God, long-term projects; spouse's siblings and sibling's spouses (in-laws)

Tenth House: Life choices, worldly and personal ambitions, officials (law and politics), bosses, career situation, rules/regulations/obstacles/aid encountered in the outer world. The mother.

Eleventh House: Results from 10th house efforts, involvement in collective activities and events, historic and collective trends and influences, groups, networks, circles of friends, connectedness, substantial gains

Twelfth House: confinement, isolation, hospitals and prisons, losses and sorrows, family problems and obligations, substantial losses; remote locations, rural income-producing property, remote income sources; bed pleasures (a Vedic house meaning that's proven relevant)

HOUSE RELATIONSHIPS

Houses have many kinds of inter-relationships that strongly influence how a twelve-house tarot spread is interpreted. House relationships determine the cards to compare for different kinds of information the client may want.

Tarotists develop individual reading styles. Generally the entire spread is laid out and examined as a whole for first impressions. I always take a few moments to soak it in and see what zones and cards stand out the most before starting an interpretation. As the reading proceeds, more details become apparent by considering the card-house relationships.

Sequential: A house relates to its neighbors - the houses before and after. This is the simplest kind of house relationship and all-important for tarotists. A card is strongly influenced by the cards on either side of it. Sequential houses emphasize the hemispheres and quadrants. Examine the whole spread for any signs of dominance: elemental, numeric, suits, Major Arcana cards, zodiacal and planetary attributions. Key clues may also come through dominant colors, recurring symbols, and images. If any of these considerations are prominent, identify the particular hemisphere or quadrant where it is most dominant.

Polarities: A house relates to the opposite house. Sometimes this can be an adversarial relationship, since opposite houses can show conflict and head-butting, or contrary priorities. Oppositions involve houses of the same modality or quadruplicity. Consider whether cards in opposition have similarities of suit, number, or attribution that help them cooperate; a lack of ties between opposing cards is likely to signify interests at odds or in conflict.

The other kind of modal relationship between houses is a square. These are three houses apart from each other. All of the pivotal-angular houses are in square or opposition relationships. All of the suceedent houses are square or opposition, as are the cadent houses. Again, similarities between cards can reduce the level of conflict, or at least identify a focal concern. For instance, if Cup cards appear in the 1st and 4th house positions, watery emotional matters are prominent in the client's life. But if a Cup is in the 1st house with a Sword card in the 4th house, there's more likely to be a level of instability or imbalance between one's personal 1st house concerns and domestic 4th house matters. Elemental dignities can be used to enormous advantage when comparing houses.

TRIPLICITIES

Triplicity relationships are triangular or trine. This is a favorable, easy house relationship. House triangles always include one angular, one suceedent, and one cadent house. There are four

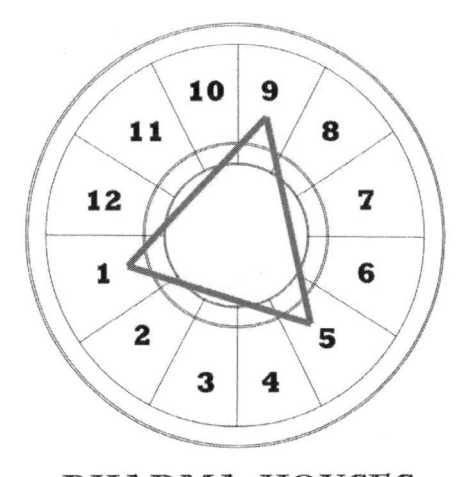

DHARMA HOUSES

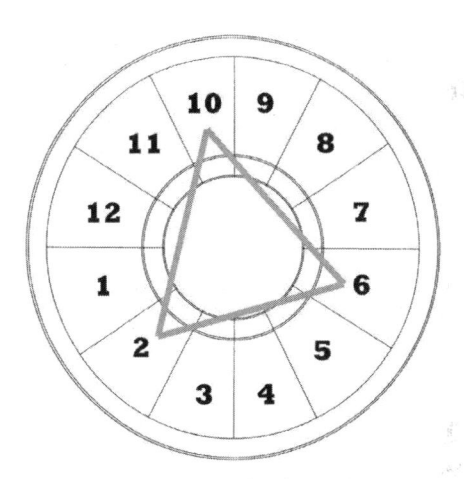

ARTHA HOUSES

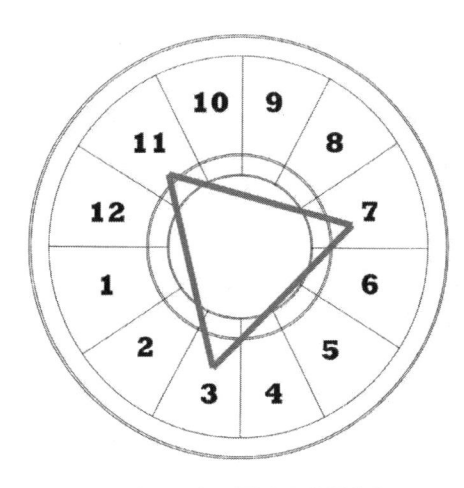

KAMA HOUSES

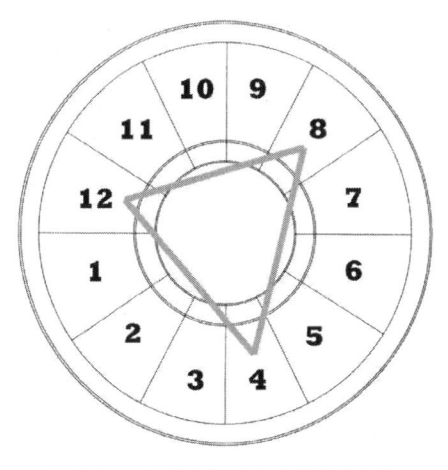

MOKSHA HOUSES

triangles in 12-house spreads. Although these are the most favorable inter-house relationships, the modal crosses are the relationships that are the most useful to assess during a tarot reading.

Vedic astrology (Jyotish, the "science of light" from India) offers lucid descriptions of the house triplicities. The **Dharma Houses** 1 – 5 – 9 are the most beneficial. They relate to one's life purpose, expression and personal development. The **Artha Houses** 2 – 6 – 10 relate to wealth and accumulation. These houses require effort but can deliver rewards. The **Kama Houses** 3 – 7 – 11 center on desires, relating and exchanges with others. The **Moksha Houses** 4 – 8 – 12 can be difficult. They relate to spirituality and enlightenment, but are also associated with the lessons one learns through family and personal hardships, difficult life lessons and misfortunes. It's far preferable to see stable cards in these houses rather than troubling ones. [1]

Houses don't exist in isolation. They are tightly intertwined by modalities, elements, polarities, and location in the numeric sequence. Tarot cards extend house relationships by suit and number. These relationships are part and parcel of house meanings. Energy flows back and forth and around the houses – it's never static. Cards placed into a 12-house form animate it with organic energy. Look for the rhythms and pulses in a 12-house spread and you won't go wrong.

All tarot spreads have a dynamic energy flow between the card positions. The energy patterns are implicit in how the spread is read and interpreted. Cards gain meaning from their neighbors. The eye can move clockwise and counter-clockwise around the 12-house circle, but also examine the polarities, quadrants, and hemispheres. There are many ways to relate cards in a 12-house spread to provide different kinds of information.

The vibrant utility of the astrological 12-house arrangement inspired Etteilla to borrow it for card readings back in the 1780s. Modern tarotists take it for granted that the cards can be placed in a twelve-house arrangement, but it took a leap of genius to borrow this from astrology and apply it to tarot. The astrological chart form provided defined position meanings and pre-fabricated inter-relationships. Why reinvent the wheel when a handy container already exists?

Written evidence of the earliest divinatory tarot methods is so spotty it's difficult to know if there were a variety of spreads in common use before the late 19th century. Large spreads with lots of cards must have been popular, or considered worth recording. The 12-house spread and the Naples arrangement both utilize a lot of cards. This is consistent with the kinds of spreads used for **LeNormand** decks, where the entire deck is laid on the table. Small tarot spreads using very few cards appear to be unique to the 20th century.

[1] James T. Braha. **Ancient Hindu Astrology for the Modern Western Astrologer**. Hermetician Press, 1986, p 37.

CHAPTER 2 REVIEW

- There are twelve houses.
- Houses have various relationships with each other including: sequential, polarities, three modalities (angular, suceedent, and cadent), and triplicities (the four elements).
- The circle contains geometric shapes: squares/crosses and triangles.
- Modalities or quadruplicities determine the relative strength of the house and its contents
- Modalities form crosses that make oppositions and squares
- Elements form triangles
- Do not conflate houses with zodiac signs and planets. Bad dog!
- The core meanings of houses have expanded over time
- The significations of a tarot card blend with the "script" provided by the topical house meanings
- Energy flows and bounces between the houses

CHAPTER 3

THE COSMIC CROSS SPREAD

This spread is included in **Tarot Decoded** because it's composed of the horizontal and vertical axes that are the main structural elements of an astrological chart and the 12-house spread. This commonly-used spread shape is included in many books with variations on how the cards are dealt into the five positions. The card positions shown here emphasize the Cosmic Cross and the way energy flows between the axis points. The spread consists of the four pivots with a central card that mediates between the polarities.

Variation 1

Card 1: The Ascendant or Self. This card shows the client's current mental, physical, and emotional conditions, and situations in the immediate environment. There may be elements of the recent past included in the significations of the card. It may show very specifically what's on the person's mind, an important concern that's the topic of the client's question.

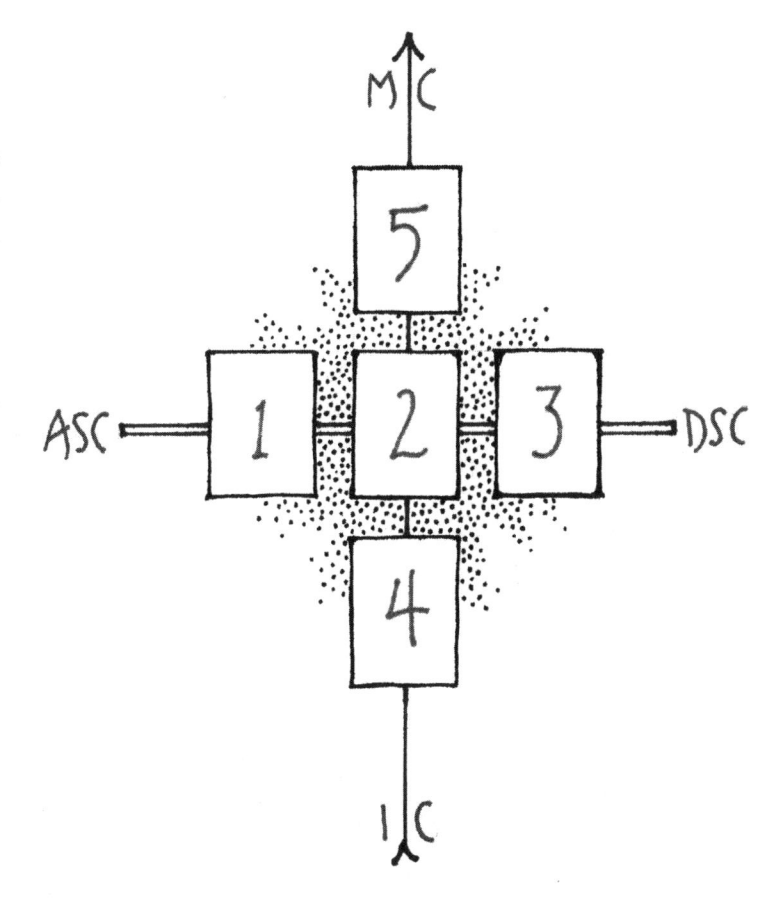

Card 2: Center-Moderator-Axle. This card shows the immediate concerns and focus, topics of central importance. It also is the unifying point of the whole spread, and acts as a moderator of the other cards. The

other four cards revolve and exchange energy around and through this central card.

Card 3: The Descendant or Other. This card shows relationships and interactions with others, along with transactions and exchanges that occupy the present and near future. The tone of this card is modified by the center card (2).

Cards 1, 2, and 3 form the horizon of the spread. The central card is an axle or fulcrum on which cards 1 and 3 are balanced like the ends of a teeter-totter. These three cards should be read as a unified group. The client (me) sits in card 1, and the client's relationship(s) sit in card 3 (others). The central card shows the mental and emotional tone of the exchanges between the client and others.

Card 4: Nadir or Foundation. This card shows the inner, private world of the client. It may describe conditions around home and family, the past, or the basis or history of the question. Evaluate this card in the context of cards 1, 2, and 3 in terms of the origins of current concerns, as well as what may be churning below the surface. The Nadir can be a refuge for hidden things, so there may be secrets and private matters lurking in this card.

Card 5: Midheaven or Outcomes. This card shows the direction the client's path will take, possibilities, outcomes, results, and the future. Major Arcana cards indicate overarching influences that may arise from internal or external sources, a dominant focus, trend or pattern. The previous four cards help define and "groom" the interpretation of the fifth card. Likewise, the fifth card may harmonize the influences shown in the previous four cards. This suggests resolutions and things being completed. It may emphasize any of the other four cards by numeric, elemental, or zodiacal relationships. Or it could be a card that has nothing whatsoever to do with the previous four cards, with a complete lack of numeric, elemental, and zodiacal connections. In this case, the cards are showing a situation, event, or condition that will emerge and override the current focus of concern. (The Tower card is notorious for upsetting apple carts in this position, as it shows things coming out of the blue and sudden upsets.)

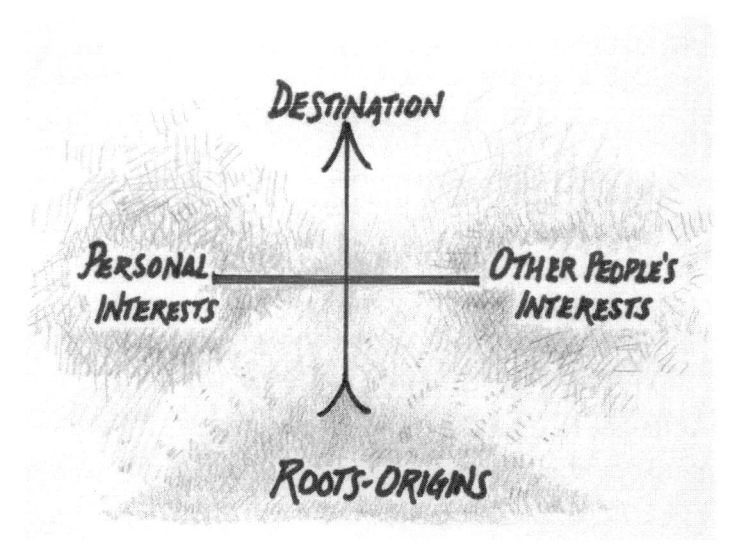

Cards 4, 2, and 5 represent the MC-IC axis. The IC is where the client is coming from, and the MC is where the client is going to. The card at the IC is modified as it encounters the horizon (card 2). The card at the MC is the usually the natural progression or outcome of what rises from the roots and intersects with the horizontal axis of encounter. The dynamic flow of energy along the horizontal and vertical axes and the modification that occurs when these axes intersect is at the core of all of the 12-house spreads. Mastering this basic spread and comprehending its dynamic flow facilitates mastering larger 12-house spreads.

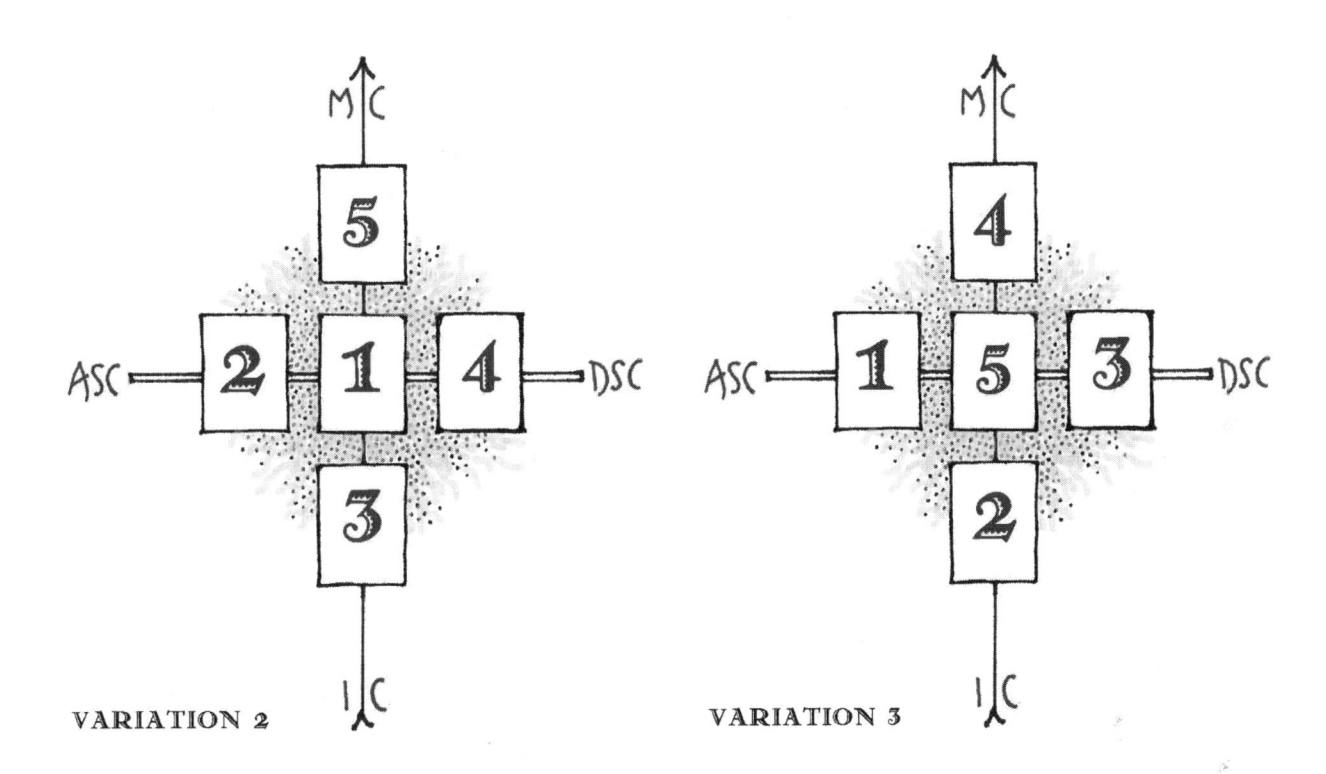

VARIATION 2

VARIATION 3

This is not the only way the cards can be placed into the five positions. Alternatives include: The position meanings remain the same; only the way the cards are dealt into these positions changes. These variations are included because they relate to the full 12-house tarot spread and variations on how that spread may be dealt.

THE CENTER CARD

The card at the center of any 12-house type spread has a big job to do. There is no equivalent of a center card in astrology – this is a cartomantic device. This card begins by showing the present, the current feelings and focus. It may represent the client's question, or something or someone that dominates client's thoughts. There can be a bit of a tussle if the client asks about one thing but is thinking about something else.

When more cards are added to a spread, the central card has a bigger job to do. It's the conduit that transmits interpretive connections from cards at the bottom of the spread (the inner hemisphere) to cards in the upper hemisphere of the 12-house spread. The movement of energy is generally from the bottom to the top, and from side-to-side. The top of the spread shows the outcomes that are (usually) the result of conditions shown by the rest of the cards.

A solitary card's meaning is static, limited by what the reader can pick up from it (and granted, this can be quite a lot depending on the reader). Placing cards next to each other creates a neighborhood. Cards that share attributions create zones of influence within a completed spread. Contiguous cards exchange energies, but contradictory or unrelated attributions and core meanings stretch the imagination and intuition.

In a 12-house spread, card connections may be generated through sequential positions, but can also stretch across the circle to entwine different houses. House-meanings provide a backdrop that allows card meanings to be heightened, changed, and modified. All spreads should perform this function. The 12-house spread performs it superbly because the house meanings are highly integrated through custom and usage.

The central card in a 12-house spread offers a meaning-full image that anchors the energies moving around the surrounding cards. A significator card performs this job to a lesser extent. The center card provides a point of reference for all of the axial relationships. A card's core and ephemeral meanings come into play when it occupies the central position. The reader should explore the card's known and potential meanings, significations, and attributions and find what works. The potential scope of a card's meanings are never more evident than when it occupies the central position.

CENTER CARD STRENGTH

The deck's structure – 22 Major Arcana cards and four suits with court and pip cards – means that some cards are automatically stronger than others and exert more impact:

- Major Arcana cards have great strength because of their profound esoteric nature and topical meanings.

- Suit cards gain strength by appearing as coalitions within a spread. Multiple cards from a particular suit make the elemental focus more dynamic (I call this "elemental dominance").

- A Major Arcana card at the center blankets the entire spread with the card's theme and client's point-of-view of the card and its influences.

Variation 1

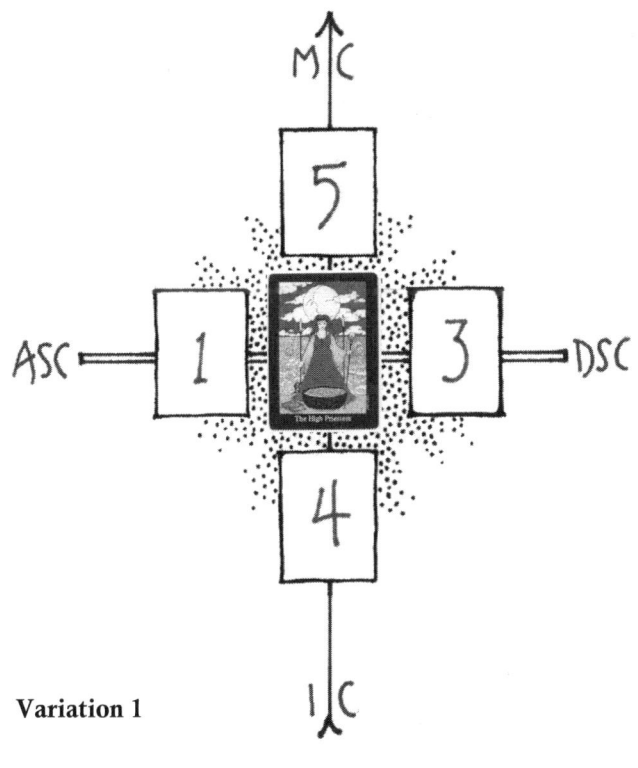

Example: if the High Priestess (2) card occupies the center, the whole spread must be considered from the standpoint of ebb and flow. At least two areas of the client's life are in transition or subject to change. Emotions can be a turbulent roller-coaster of highs and lows. Current and future event cycles will skew to the Moon's new and full phases. There's a powerful impulse to periodically stop, shut down the external noise, and take time for inner reflection and emotional processing. The client may regard ongoing events as a part of a larger process, and temper knee-jerk reactions with wisdom. One of the benefits of the High Priestess as a central card is that things indicated by the surrounding cards flow through her unhindered; that's one of her main qualities. The client may be a keen observer of what's going on around her, well aware that things in her life are in a process of transition.

Another Example: if the Devil (15) is in the center, the limitations and compulsions it represents for the client dominate all other considerations in the reading. Potentially good opportunities indicated by the surrounding cards can be ham-strung by the liabilities imposed by the Devil. For example, if the client works in a mega-corporation with a toxic corporate culture, or in a bureaucracy that's rife with corruption (not-uncommon meanings for the Devil), the influence of the work situation can taint everything else in that person's life. Alcoholism, co-dependence, chronic illness, indebtedness, and heavy family burdens can have the same effect. Only another powerful Major Arcana card can mitigate the influence of the Devil. The Hierophant could suggest that the client is reaching toward spirituality to offset hard realities through a connection with the divine. If the Hierophant occupies one of the pivots, it has more power to offset a central Devil card.

The Devil
from **The Whispering Tarot**

A central suit card, whether a court or a pip card, doesn't have the pervasive influence of a Major Arcana card. As in poker or euchre, a central suit card accumulates more power in the spread through alliances and affinities. Allied cards in any house may contribute to a central card's capacity to mediate cards in the surrounding houses; allied cards in the pivots give a big boost to the center card.

Court cards have a different function from the numbered pip cards. A central king or queen concentrates personal qualities and traits. Knights and princess-pages are better behaved and more focused when there's a king or queen (of any suit) in the spread to supervise; a same-suit court card is best. A central pip card becomes more active with a same-suit court card to bring the meanings into manifestation. Nobody spews verbal abuse from the 3 of Swords like the Knight of Swords! This is a negative example, but the principle of affinity isn't limited to rainbows, kittens and puppies. Tough cards get tougher and good cards get better when there are same-suit cards linked to the central card.

Numeric connections also help a center card. Multiples of any numeric designation (like three Aces) underscores the esoteric meaning of that number. Since these cards don't share an elemental connection, the number signifies similar things occurring in different areas of life. If the central card shares a number with cards in houses, the number's relevance is heightened.

Example: if the center card is the 2 of Cups, and the 2 of Swords and 2 of Wands are in the houses, it suggests a prominent theme of one-on-one conversations about possibilities. Separate situations may have parallel elements. The qualities of duality and efforts to establish balance are emphasized. Twos are early in the numeric series so are tentative and exploratory. There may not be much for the client to work with unless higher numbered cards of the same suit contribute further developments.

The central card works best when it can operate as a multi-tasker. The relative power of the card (Major Arcana, court, or pip card) determines how much the card needs the support of affinities with the surrounding house cards. A central card that has **no** numeric, elemental, or astrological affinities with the rest of the spread is isolated or alienated from its surroundings. It has to operate without allies. This in itself may be an accurate reflection of a client's current state. The client may *feel* isolated or disconnected from what's going on in her life. Thoughts and feelings may be anomalous or irrelevant to what's going on in the environment, like a "rebel without a clue."

In another respect, the client's central focus may be totally unrelated to current events. This can be a very uncomfortable reading for the reader to give. An isolated central card turned up in a reading for a client I read for a few years ago. She was obsessed with a past love relationship and hoped this man would return. Since the central card had no affinities with the surrounding cards, a reunion was highly unlikely. Other important issues were described by the surrounding cards, but the client returned again and again to the topic of her lost lover.

An unrelated central card is comparable to a ***consideration before judgment***, a useful concept I'm borrowing from horary astrology. There are particular considerations before judgment that make a horary chart unreadable, thus unable to answer the question asked of the astrologer. Simply stated: the chart is a dud or a lemon. Likewise, an unrelated central card in a full 12-house spread is going to be rare, because there are so many cards in the spread. It's a red flag that the client's central concerns are not in sync with the surrounding cards. An unrelated central card in the five-card Cosmic Cross spread isn't as problematic. The odds of an unrelated card are much greater in a smaller spread. It could simply indicate that the client is hoping for something exciting to happen, while the card in the fourth house shows that there are plumbing problems that need immediate attention. The reader has to determine the extent of the dissociation with surrounding events.

There's always an exception to the rule; in this case, it's the Major Arcana cards attributed to planets. Planets can and do go everywhere and relate to everything. The example given above, the High Priestess, is attributed to the Moon. The Moon is reflective, so the High Priestess can absorb or transfer anything shown in the surrounding cards. If a Major Arcana planet-attributed card occupies the center of a 12-house type spread, it suggests that the client is interacting with the surrounding situations with the particular qualities and traits of the card/planet.

Anything that helps define the central card is a clue that helps the reader dig into its layers of meaning. The clues may include affinities and connections with the surrounding cards, but it can also be the complete lack of them.

If a central card has no numeric or elemental affinities (which include zodiacal connections by element), then it might share a planetary attribution with other cards. *Example*: The 6 of Swords, 5 of Pentacles, and 3 of Cups share no numeric or elemental affinities, but they are all Mercury cards in the Golden Dawn attribution system. Readers may also use attributions based on the Kabalistic Tree of Life's Sephiroth attributions, including the 22 paths that link the trump cards, and the connections between the Sephiroth and the court cards.

CHAPTER 3 REVIEW

- The position meanings of the Cosmic Cross spread always are the same
- The cards can be placed into the positions in various ways
- The Cosmic Cross consists the ASC-DSC and MC-IC axes
- The central card moderates the four surrounding cards
- The central card in any 12-house type spread operates on multiple levels

- A central card that's a suit card (court or pip) gains strength through alliances and affiliations with surrounding cards
- A central Major Arcana card influences the entire spread
- A central card that lacks shared attributions with surrounding cards may indicate alienation, or that the client is focused on something irrelevant to what's actually happening his his or her present situation.
- A Major Arcana card attributed to a planet in the center can relate to anything around it; it benefits from affiliations but doesn't need them.

CHAPTER 4

VARIATION 1: THE SEQUENTIAL TWELVE-HOUSE SPREAD

This is the most commonly-known version of this spread and the one that's usually provided in tarot books. The cards are spread sequentially in house order. The central card may be placed first or last. Or the reader may choose to use a significator card. Significator cards are an antique convention that seems to be disappearing in tarot practice.

Illustrations of three sequential spreads are given below. Feel free to experiment with the variations; there is no "best" version. Figure out what works best for you. The cards in the pivots are straight up and down, which makes them look most powerful (which they are).

One advantage of starting with the center card as shown in Variation 2 is the option to add a final (14th) card to cover it at the end of the spread for further clarification.

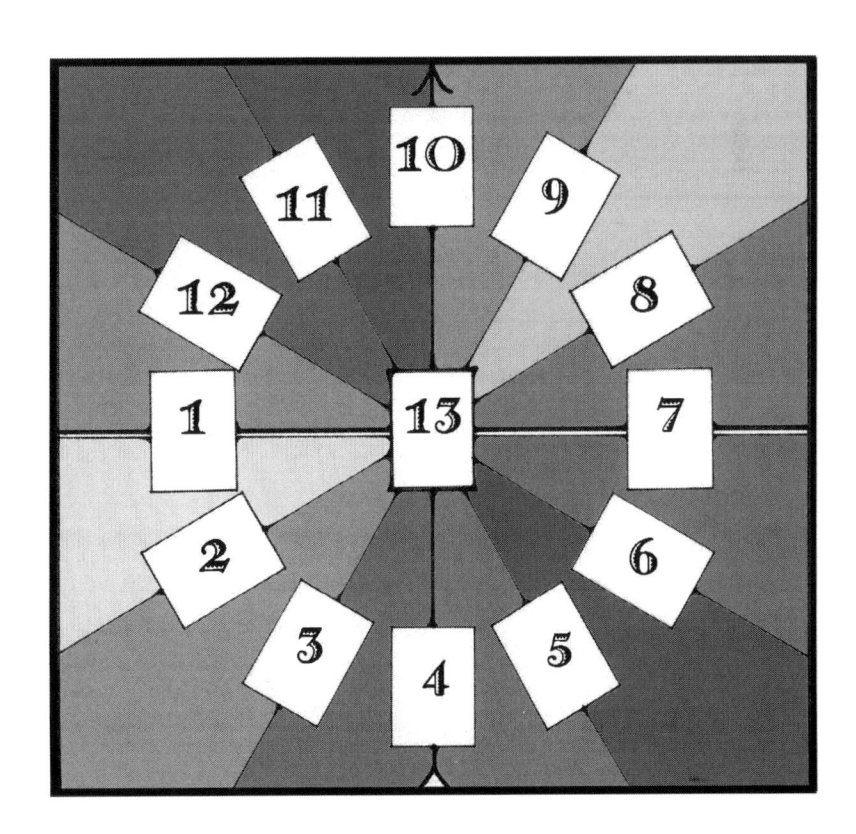

Sequential –Version 1

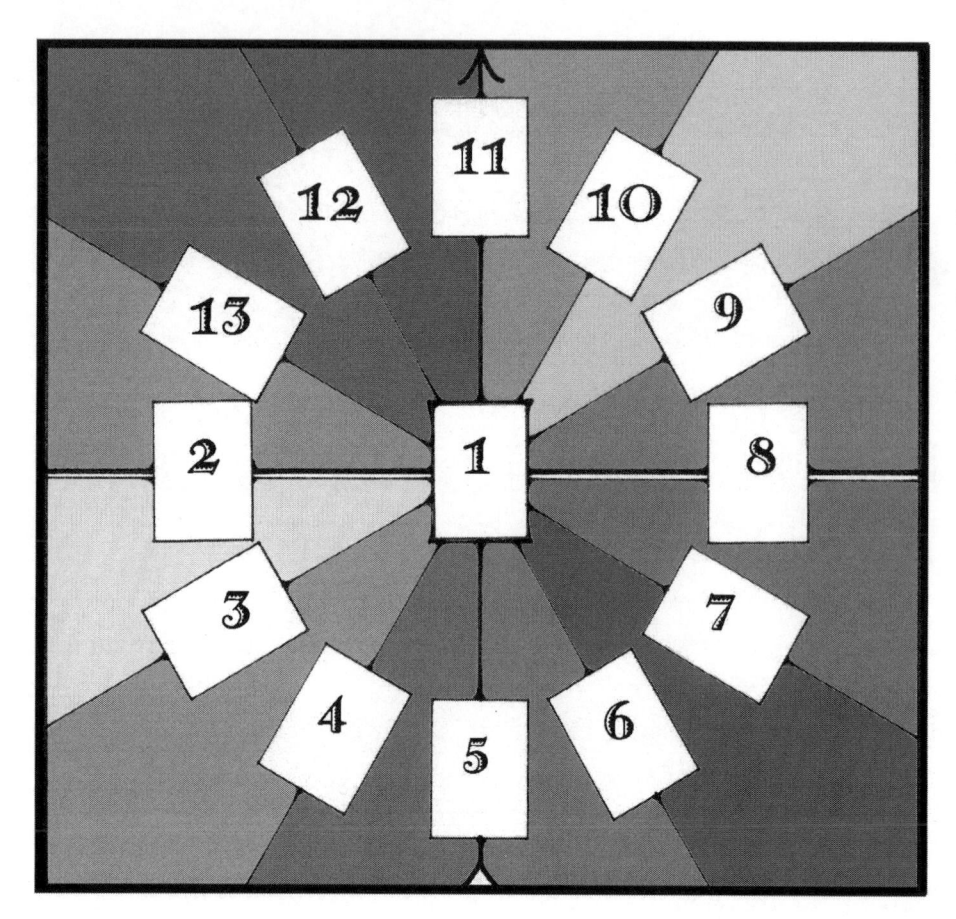

Sequential—Version 2

Begin with Card 1 in the center

Card 2 is placed in the first house; deal cards sequentially. Card 13 is in the 12th house.

The sequential 12-house spread is often used for **topical readings**. Topical readings are simply an overview of topics: relationships, health, finances, family life, children, love affairs, etc. Below is a list of which houses relate to specific topics:

Relationships: 1st, 7th, 5th, 11th, sometimes 3rd.
Finances: 2nd and 8th, sometimes 4th, 11Th, and 12th
Career: 10th and 6th, with influences from the 2nd and 11th.
Family: 4th, 3rd, 6th, 9th, 12th.
Children: 5th and 11th.
Love affairs: 5th, 7th, and 11th; sometimes 12th.
Health: 1st, 6th, sometimes with 8th and 12th (these may refer to other people's health matters).
Travel and Education: 3rd and 9th, sometimes 11th.
Religion and Spirituality: 9th, 8th, 12th, and sometimes 4th.
Hidden Matters: 12th, 4th, 6th, and 8th.
Inheritances: 4th and 8th.
Pets: traditionally 6th, but modern use favors the 5th. Large animals (bigger than a goat) are 12th.
Karmic issues: 4th, 8th, 12th, 1st.

Connect and blend the meanings of the cards in the topical houses to provide answers. For example, if a client asks about finances, look at the cards in the 2nd and 8th house positions. The 2nd house shows skills and possessions and the 8th house shows what is received in exchange for those skills, along with changes associated with the partner, family or employer that may impact money matters. The 4th house represents accumulated family wealth, particularly property. The 11th house can show raises, promotions and bonuses (but a card in this position may not necessarily do so). A card in the 12th house may show income from remote locations. This could be income generated through telecommuting or an internet business, or from land or houses (income-producing properties) the client owns but does not occupy. It could also be money from the sale of inherited properties. If a card like the 4 of Pentacles appears in the 12th house, it could well refer to remote income sources. A lot of factors can influence a person's financial status.

Cards of the same suit or element can link house topics, too. The 3rd and 8th houses aren't connected by modality or triplicity. But if the 7 of Wands is in the 3rd house and the 3 of Wands in the 8th house, there may be somewhat stressful conversations with a partner about possible deals and opportunities. Or perhaps new potential sources of income are available through others (the 8th), but the client is already bogged down with too much to do. The 3rd house relates to daily movements and the 7 of Wands indicates the client is struggling to keep up with current responsibilities. Houses occupied by cards with shared attributions automatically have some kind of dialog.

The reader may choose to read a sequential spread sequentially, describing each house in numeric order without particularly integrating card meanings. This is an acceptable method for learning the house meanings. The reader can ask the client to choose one or two topics of interest, and examine the relevant houses for information.

Worksheets with the sequential 12-house variations are provided at the end of the book for the reader's convenience. Use these to copy down the spread and make notes about card significations for each house.

NEW YEAR'S SPREAD

The sequential spread works well for 12-month forecasts. Some readers use this spread around New Year's or in early January to make predictions for the coming year, but it can be used this way at any time.

The card in the 1st house represents the current month, or the beginning of the period in question. This diagram shows January in the 1st house, but the reading can start with any month. It can also be divided into different time units. Each quadrant can be a week or a month, or even into the twelve hours of a day.

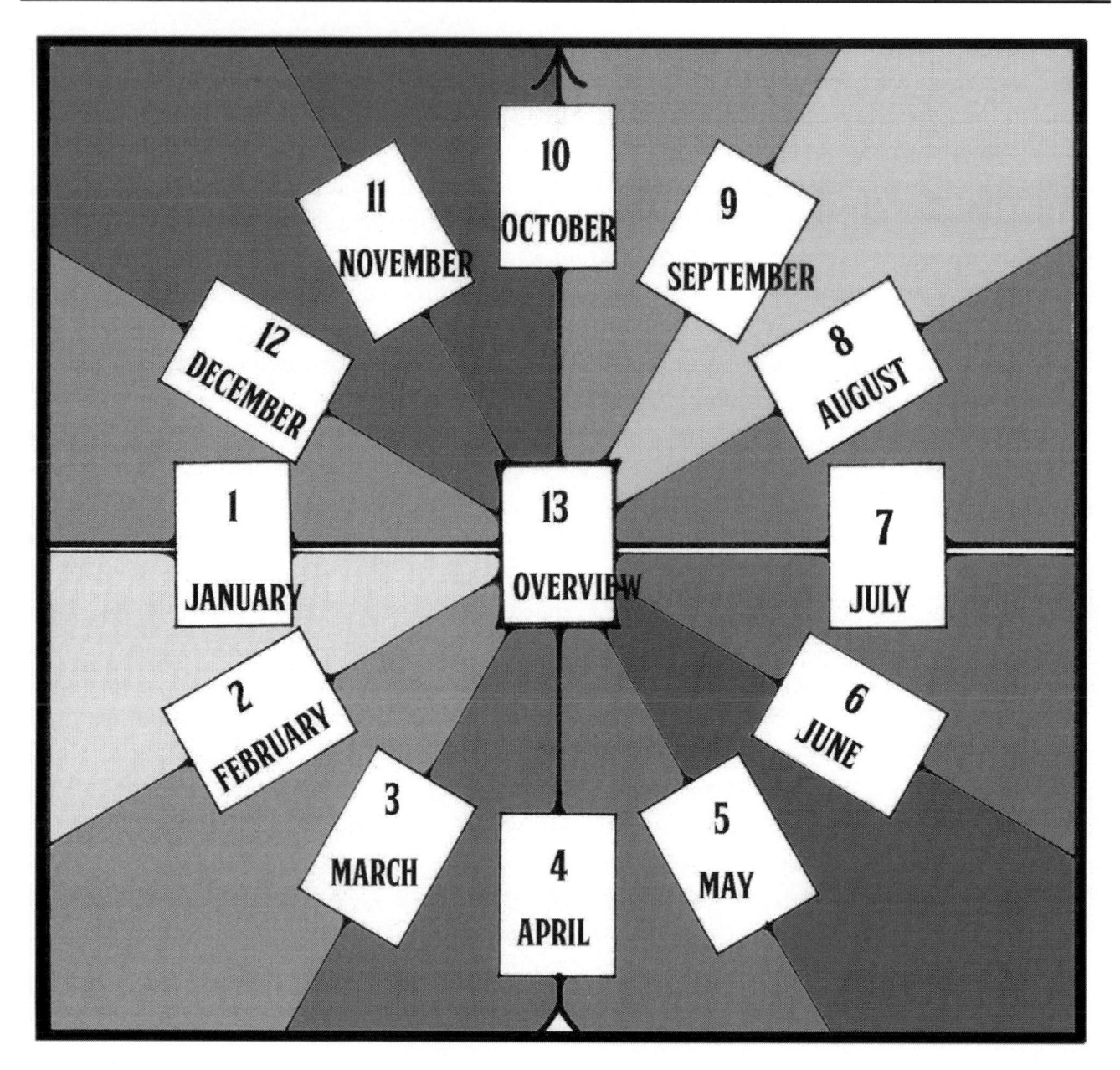

Sequential—Version 3
New Year's Spread

Card 1 is in the first house and represents the first month (week, or day). Complete the spread by placing Card 13 in the center.

Any month or designated time period can occupy the first house.

The sequential 12-house spread is useful to astrologers, too. It can be combined with a solar return chart (i.e., the predictive annual birthday chart erected for the exact moment the transiting

Sun is at the degree and minute it occupied at the person's moment of birth) to augment insights into the client's year ahead. This works best if the solar return is used as a stand-alone chart without a biwheel or triwheel. Compare the solar return's planetary placements and focal houses to the cards in the 12-house spread. Take note of the house positions occupied by Major Arcana cards. If the Major Arcana card is attributed to a Zodiac sign, check which house in the chart has that sign on the cusp in a solar return. What house does that sign's ruling planet occupy and what aspects is it making? If a Major Arcana card is attributed to a planet, find the planet in the solar return chart and assess its condition by sign, house and aspects. Check which house[s] that planet rules.

If there's a Court card, figure out who it represents. When using this technique, Court cards almost always represent a specific person rather than personal characteristics. The card's house position might be the clue, but check the solar return house cusps for the Court card's elemental attribution. The client may know right away who this person is if the Court card's qualities are described, too. In that case, the house position tells what activity connects the client and that person. For instance, if a Queen occupies the third house position, they could be traveling or talking on a daily basis in the coming year. The third house indicates frequent interactions.

A 12-house spread is a fantastic supplement to a forecasting chart like a solar return. The card images can give a great deal of insight into what areas of life will be of most concern in the coming year, as well as explaining more about existing situations, the client's feelings about those conditions, and about interpersonal dynamics at work in the chart. It's amazing how often using a 12-house spread with a solar return chart can set the reader on the right interpretive track. Sometimes tarot cards can even point out what to look for in a chart! The cards are uncanny, and usually (in my experience) give signals to look for things in the chart that may have been overlooked. Combining these methods makes them stronger, more dynamic, and best of all, more accurate.

If the astrologer wants to experiment, combine the card in the first house position with the chart's first house and read them together for that person's month of birth. Follow it with the second house card and chart's second house for the second month, etc. If there's no planet in the house, look at the condition of planet that rules the sign on the cusp. This forecasting method provides a glimpse at the next twelve months of the client's life.

CHAPTER 5

VARIATION 2: THE POLARITY TWELVE-HOUSE SPREAD

This arrangement focuses on the six house polarities. The central card is key to moderating or refereeing the oppositions. There are placement options: the center card can be placed first, second, or last.

Polarity—Version 1

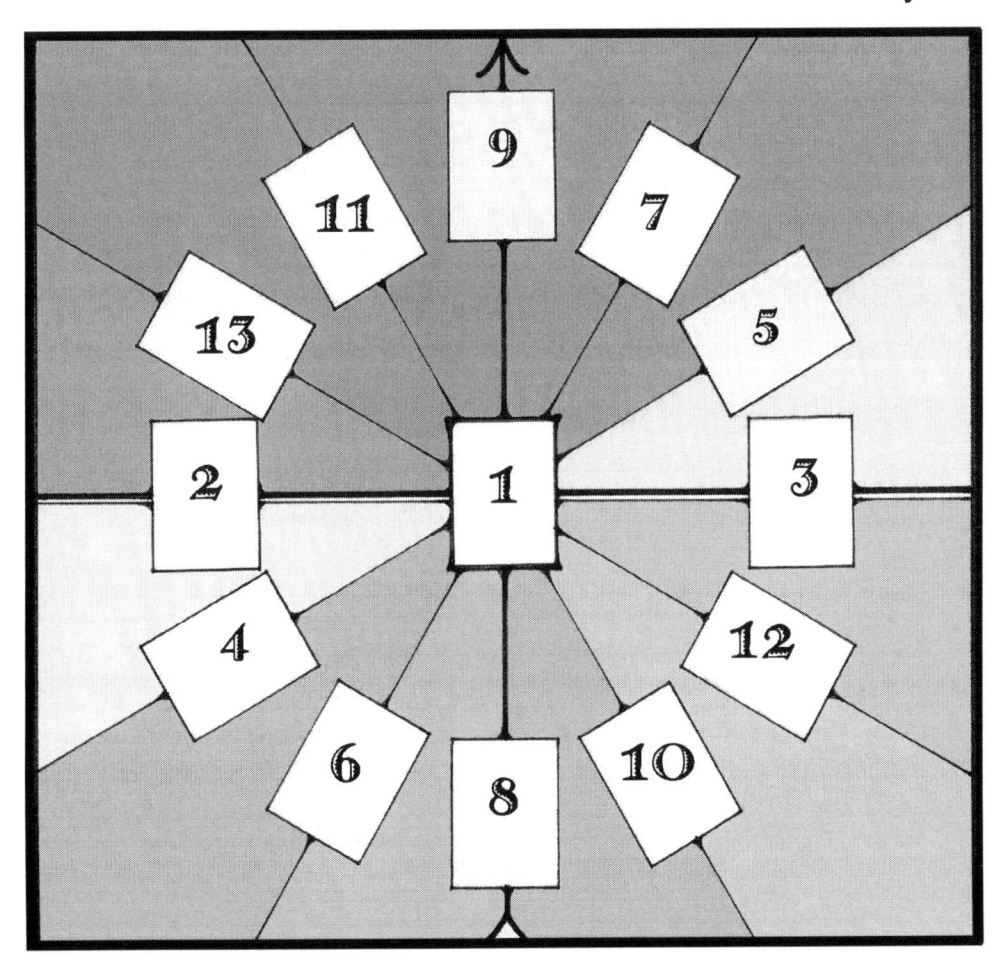

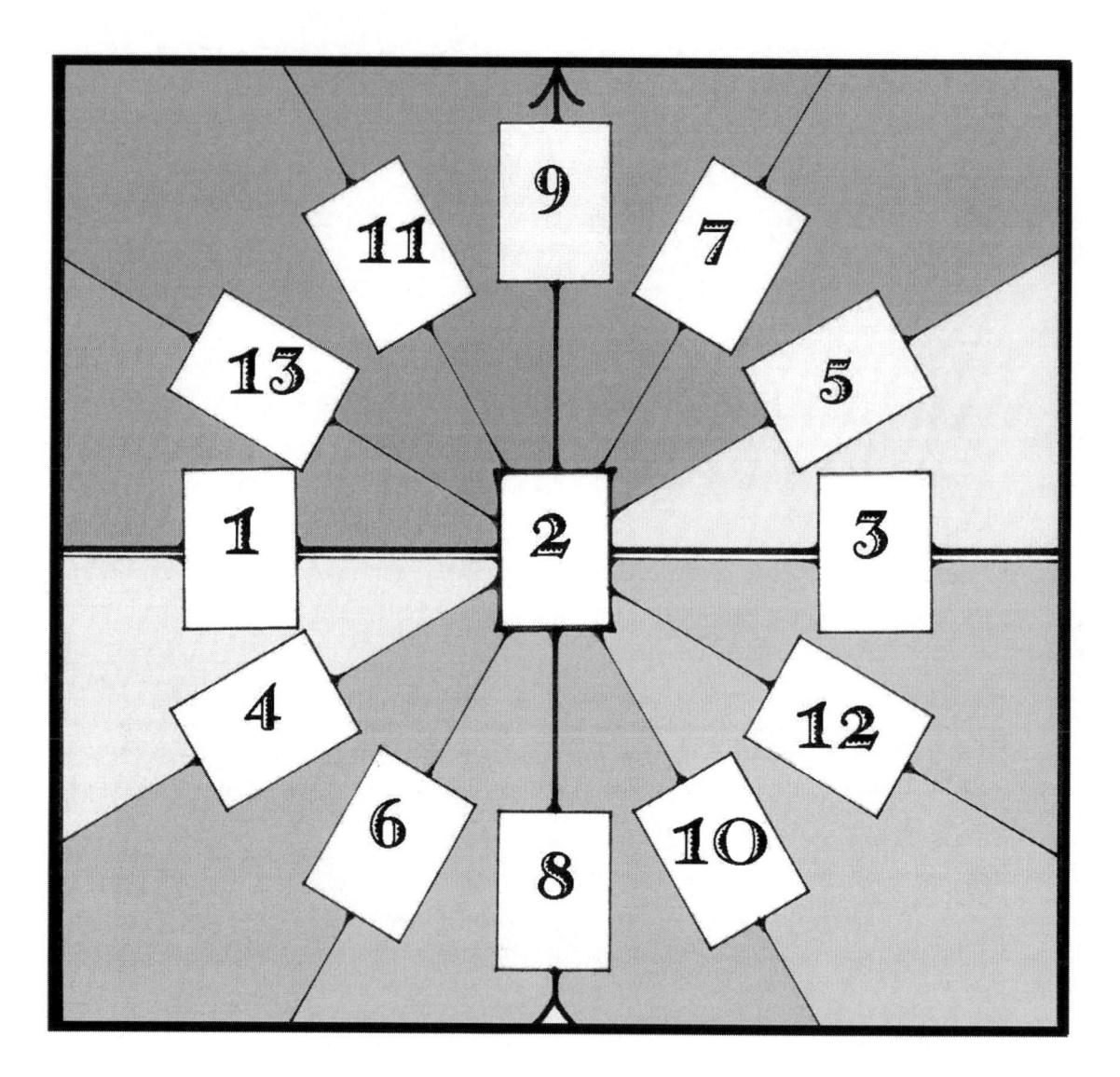

Polarity—Version 2

The first card is placed in the 1st house

The second card is placed in the center position

The third card is placed in the 7th house

The fourth card is placed in the 2nd house, etc.

Variation 2: The Polarity Twelve-House Spread

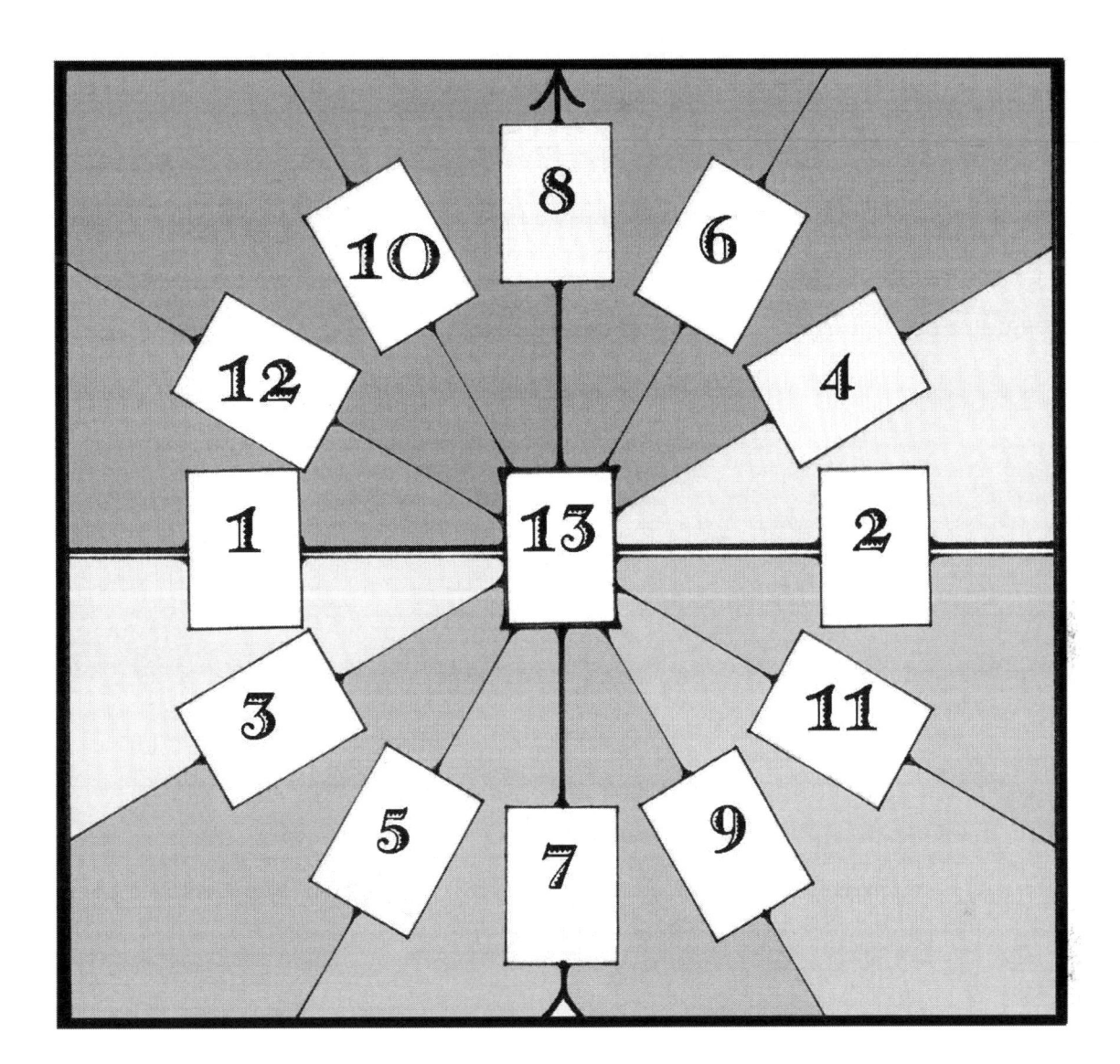

Polarity—Version 3

The first card is placed in the 1st house

The second card is placed in the 7th house

The third card is placed in the 2nd house, fourth card in the 8th house, etc.

The thirteenth card is placed in the final center position.

Polarity 12-house variations are useful for clients who want to focus on their primary relationship. The cards in houses 1 through 6 represent the client; the cards in houses 7 through 12 represent the partner. Polarity spreads are helpful for clients engaged in making important decisions, since the polarities can show the pros and cons of different aspects of a decision.

When working with the 12-house polarity spread for a relationship reading, the bottom six houses represent the client; the top six houses represent the client's partner. The cards in the 1st and 7th houses show prominent personality traits and feelings. The cards in the 2nd and 8th houses signify each partner's value system regarding finances and assets, and the balance of give-and-take between the partners.

The cards in the 3rd and 9th houses show how the partners communicate with each other. Court cards here could show people who help or hinder the relationship, a person who is a topic of discussions, or even traits that help or hurt communications. The cards in the 4th and 10th houses show goals; consider if the cards show shared or similar goals, or goals that are contrary to the other partner's goals. This house may also show issues around the home, family members, and real-estate.

The cards in the 5th and 11th houses, shown above as "sex or independence," shows how well the partners relate to each other physically in loving ways, and whether or not they're able to give each other space to be independent, have their own friends, or have time alone. The cards in the 6th and 12th houses, "work or health," can show working conditions and health matters. There may be hidden issues or secrets that the other partner isn't aware of.

Polarity Spread for a Relationship Reading

The central card is the bridge between the partners. It may show overarching influences, a topic of contention or a shared interest. Any of the variations of the polarity spread can be used for a relationship reading. If the reader uses Variation III, the final 13th card can be reserved until the end of the reading as a summation card.

If the reader is doing this spread for a couple, have each partner draw six cards from a fanned deck. Place one partner's cards into the bottom six positions, and the other partner's cards into the top six positions. Let each partner draw one final card at the end of the reading for a summation. The house meanings remain the same, but changing the way cards are dealt into house positions intensifies the relationship between cards in opposite houses. Each polarity has a topical focus:

House Polarity Meanings

1st and 7th   relationships, one-on-one exchanges, spouse or partner

2nd and 8th   money and finances, value systems, give-and-take, trust issues

3rd and 9th   daily flow of activities, long-term planning, communications

4th and 10th   home life and career; past conditions and future choices, family and home

5th and 11th   relationships with friends, children, creative efforts, sex and independence

6th and 12th   working conditions, physical health, and hidden issues

Consider if the cards on either side of a polarity (or opposition) are friendly, neutral, or inimical. Friendly cards can be cards with positive meanings, or cards that share elemental, zodiacal, or numeric attributions. If a pip card is on one side and a Major Arcana card is in opposition, the house with the Major Arcana card exerts a lot more power. The issues of the Major Arcana card's house position may overwhelm the card in the opposite house. A shared number or element card could show how the partner supports the other.

Court cards get an interpretive boost since house positions relate to specific people. A court card in the 7th house is very likely a partner or an individual of primary importance to the client. The 3rd house shows siblings or friends one meets on a daily basis. The 4th house shows family members, the 5th house lovers, friends, and children. The 6th house is co-workers and sometimes a spouse that works at home or works with the client. The 9th house shows in-laws, cousins, teachers and ministers. The 10th house shows bosses and people in positions of power; the 11th house shows professional acquaintances and good friends in social settings. The 12th house can be a little strange – it can show relatives in distress, health care professionals and healers, or even hidden affairs. This is a sketchy list of how the court cards may be personified by house position. Studying house meanings provides plenty of options for eliciting very specific descriptions of the people the court cards represent in their lives and the roles they play.

Example: The 7 of Cups in the center, Ace of Wands in the 5th house, and the Queen of Swords in the 11th house. *Instant clue*: None of these cards share numbers, elements, or zodiacal attributions. The Ace and Queen have some affinity as fire and air cards but the 7 of Cups muddles up their relationship. The 7 of Cups is emotionally unstable and changeable. Its attribution is Venus/Scorpio. Venus doesn't relate well to Scorpio since it's her sign of detriment. It's an awkward fit;

she has to work a lot harder and doesn't belong in the environment. Think of a woman wearing a ball gown and diamond tiara at a football game (she's not the homecoming queen, either). Venus's wants and needs are jostled by exterior considerations, realities, and the inherent limitations of Scorpio. Her desires are at odds or are unavailable and force her to consider alternatives and options.

This is why the seven cups are filled with all sorts of different things. It's tough for Venus to choose and make commitments to these alternative possibilities. If the client is exceptionally good at making lemonade out of lemons (or if she's a Scorpio), this card isn't as problematic. The trick is spotting or maximizing the potential of lesser options.

The 7 of Cups shows the client isn't fully invested in what's going on in the polarities of the twelve houses. There's some waffling and uncertainty, and perhaps a bit of resistance to making necessary adjustments until things line up perfectly. Venus wants perfection, and this planet can feel a bit grubby and Second-Hand Rose in Scorpio if nothing else supports her there. What other people say and do has a greater impact on the client. No matter what cards occupy the pivots, the client could flounder in her own diffidence.

The 7 of Cups makes a tippy, wobbly fulcrum at the center. It's up to the reader to determine through the reading process if the client is wobbly by nature, if the client has been thrust into a wobbly period of life and doesn't know what to choose, or if things are changing around her so quickly that her response is to wobble with uncertainty.

The Ace of Wands in the 5th house shows a burst of creativity. It's a fiery card in a dharma house. It can mean some kind of conception. A pregnancy is a possibility, but it could also be a spark of a new ambition that stimulates (or rises from) the client's creative, original thoughts. On a very physical level, this trio of cards could signify a pregnancy that presents a whole new spectrum of future considerations to the client; the Queen of Swords would be an OB/GYN giving assistance and practical information.

The Queen of Swords in the 11th house is an airy card in an kama house. She isn't very friendly to the 7 of Cups or the Ace of Wands. She holds a sword of truth or decision-making in her hand. She has strong opinions about what will or won't work in the real world, and she occupies the outer world quadrant. She has strong critical skills and cuts to the heart of the matter when giving advice.

The client has a new ambition (Ace) but can't fully commit to it (7 of Cups) until she runs through some kind of gauntlet (Qu Sw). Maybe the client shares her inspirations with a friend who gives or withholds approval. This friend may suggest methods that edit and refine the original idea.

In another respect, the client may be full of great ideas but won't follow through out of fear of disapproval. She may imagine all sorts of obstacles (7 of Cups) so allows her ideas (Ace of Wands) to wither on the vine rather than face criticism or lack of full acceptance (Queen of Swords). Maybe the client has already presented an article (Ace) to an editor (Queen), and received suggestions about how to improve it. With the 7 of Cups in the center, her feelings may be hurt or she may feel insulted that her article isn't immediately accepted as golden prose.

The Queen of Swords could even be an inner critic blocking and discouraging free expression. Depending on your reading style, you may want to start with the idea that the Queen is a real person that the client has to satisfy in some way, and there's an intimidation factor. The Ace of Wands is jubilant but kind of spastic and combustible; the Queen is thoughtful and precise. The Queen of Swords will want to cobble the Ace's spark into something useful and sophisticated that can be conveyed to others.

CHAPTER 6

VARIATION 3: THE SPIRAL TWELVE-HOUSE SPREAD

Spiral layout patterns further integrate the ways that energy flows through the twelve houses. There are options for placing the first five cards. Version 1 follows the spiraling principle throughout the arrangement. Version 2 mimics the original Cosmic Cross Spread. Both versions place the central card at the beginning of the spread.

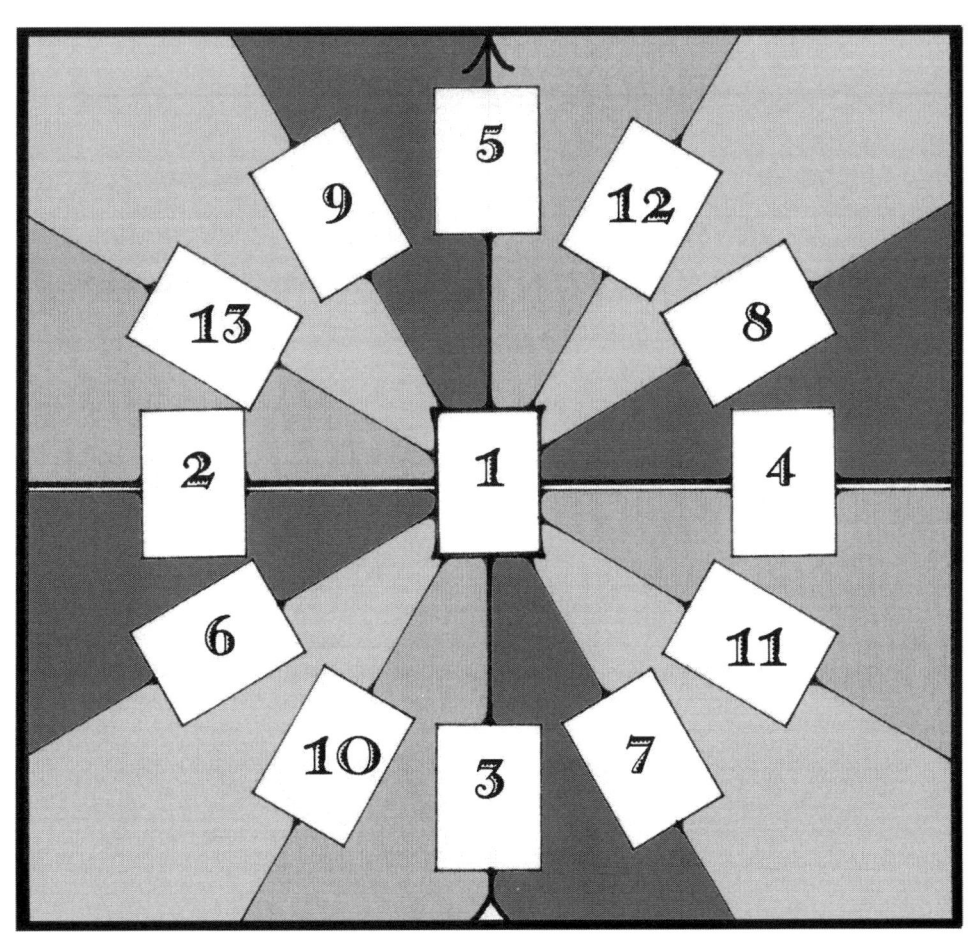

Spiral—Version 1

Card 1 in Center
Card 2 in 1st house
Card 3 in 4th house
Card 4 in 7th house
Card 5 in 10th house

Card 6 in the 2nd house, etc.

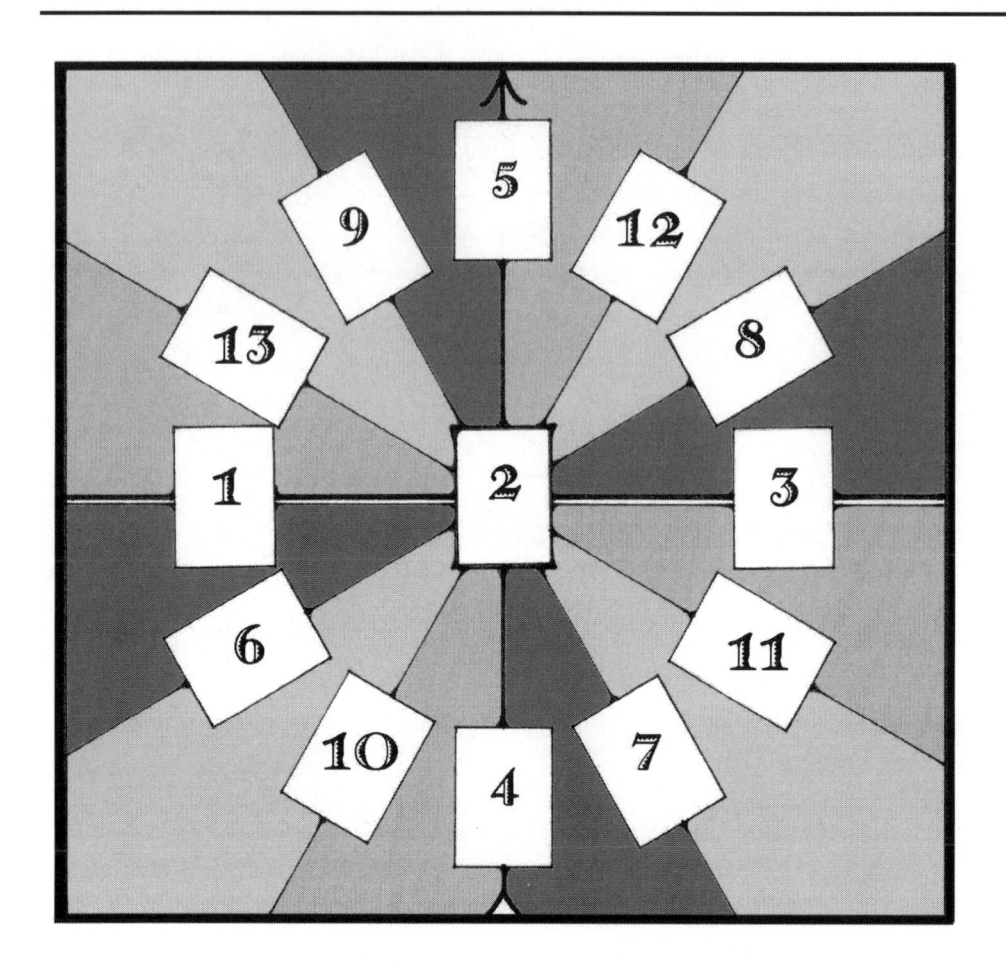

Spiral—Version 2

Card 1 in 1st house
Card 2 in Center
Card 3 in 7th house
Card 4 in 4th house
Card 5 in 10th house

Card 6 in 2nd house, etc.

Spiral spread patterns underscore the dynamic quadruplicity relationships between the angular, suceedent, and cadent houses. The cards in the three modal crosses are tightly integrated in spiral spreads. The first five cards from the deck are in the pivots, in the strongest positions in the spread. As an older witch and tarotist told me many years ago, "Falls to the floor, close to the door; right at the top, ready to pop."

Cards 6 – 7 – 8 – 9 occupy the suceedent cross and are moderately strong. The matters attributed to the suceedent houses are less likely to change; relationships (5th and 11th) tend to be lasting. Finances are generally stable (2nd – 8th). When momentous cards land in these polarities and are supplemented by equally potent cards in the pivots, significant adjustments are likely.

Consider what's likely to work well in the suceedent house positions. Its good to see positive earthy cards like the 3 of Pentacles or 10 of Pentacles in the 2nd and 8th (money) houses. The 5th and 11th house positions favor cards like the 4 of Wands, 6 of Wands, the 6 of Swords, the Aces and Pages, as cards like these relate to happy relationships, social enjoyment, creativity, messages and invitations, and interesting new things to pursue.

As in previous spreads, look for numbers and suits that support each other and link the matters indicated by the houses, even if the houses don't have critical angular relationships.

Example: the Knight of Pentacles is in the 6th house and the 3 of Pentacles is in the 11th house. Working groups (6th house knight) that are efficient and dedicated will get rewards for effort (results-oriented 11th).

Example: if Cups cards are in the 2nd, 4th, and 9th houses, the client may be preparing for reunions and travels that relate to family matters. The Cups suit links the house meanings. The cards add details. Let's say the 2 of Cups is in the 2nd house, the 8 of Cups in the 4th, and the 3 of Cups in the 9th. The 2 of Cups indicates discussing or sharing 2nd house financial resources. The 8 of Cups shows thoughts of the past, of family members at a distance, or perhaps some disappointments with the planning process. Maybe the timing is inconvenient, forcing the client to choose between priorities. The 3 of Cups suggests a celebration is the reason for a 9th house journey. The 9th house specifies cousins, a spouse's siblings, or even friends who live in distant places.

The energy bounces around between the houses and cards. Numbers can link houses in the same way.

Example: The Hanged Man (12, 1 + 2 = 3) in the 12th house, and the 3 of Swords in the 3rd house. The number 3 links the cards. Three is a fertile number, but these are rotten cards! There's more pain to go around. Deaths sometimes happen in threes. Multiple uncontrollable problems could come up; the 3 of Swords can relate to gizmos on the fritz, traffic jams or getting stuck in a grocery store line. All the Hanged Man can do is sit and stare. Or listen to some soothing music and meditate. The 3rd house relates to siblings and day-to-day exchanges, while the 3 of Swords indicates sorrows, lawsuits, betrayal, and losses. A sibling could lose a job or have serious health or legal issues. This might apply to someone the client talks to on a daily basis. The Hanged Man underscores the significations of the 12th house: confinement, hospitals, prisons, loss and helplessness, family problems with karmic debts. The Hanged Man augurs sacrifices and situations where waiting and praying are the only thing to do.

The 3 of Swords is a Saturn/Libra card, and the Hanged Man is Water/Neptune. Saturn and Neptune break down old structures and familiar relationships, and the conditions surrounding those relationships. The daily patterns and relationships of the 3rd house are in upheaval.

A reader seeing a combination like this has to make a choice about how to deliver the interpretation. The client may already be aware of the things the cards are showing. The 3rd and 12th houses are cadent, so the cards here are weaker. There may be big trouble, but it isn't the client's trouble; somebody else is caught up in a shit storm. The Hanged Man has all the power of a Major Arcana card, though. It looms over the card in the Ascendant and its influence leaks into the first house. The trouble described by this card has been around for a while. The client may have given up on trying to intervene or assist.

Finishing the Spread

One more spiral can be added to this spread. The reader can choose whether to place these on the table with the other cards or to reserve these final cards until the main spread has been interpreted. The five cover cards offer clarification and additional information about the future. Place the cover cards the same way as shown below for both Variation 1 and 2 spiral spreads.

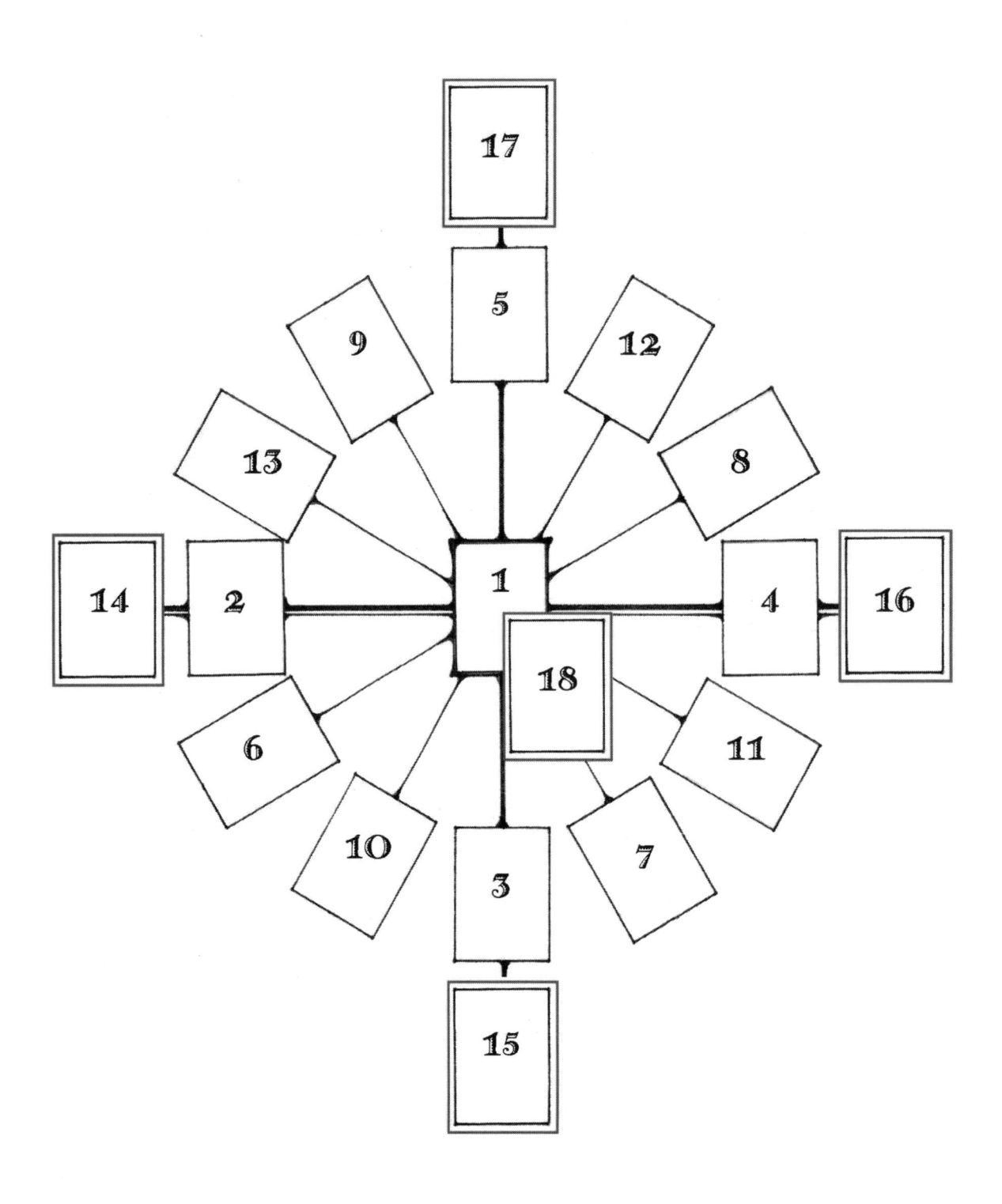

Variation 3: The Spiral Twelve-House Spread

This is an elegant, in-depth spread that's fabulous for a half-hour or hour-long reading. This arrangement offers plenty of information about every area of life.

All of the methods described in the previous 12-house spread variations work with this spread. The cards can be read sequentially starting from the card in the first house position moving counter-clockwise around the spread. The reader can describe areas of life in a topical manner by linking the cards in houses that have related subjects. The spread can be analyzed using the triplicity house relationships described on page 21, and by using the polarities shown on page 16. The modal house relationships described on pages 17-18 are of particular note because this spiral spread arrangement highlights these card relationships. The cards in the pivotal houses (1—4—7—10) are of the greatest importance.

This spread can be combined very effectively with astrological charts like a solar return or a tri-wheel with current progressions and transits. It can be used to augment a Draconic chart interpretation if the client wants to focus on questions about life-long karmic issues.

Proceed by reading the cards in small sections. Examine the contents of each quadrant. Look at cards in the 1st, 2nd, and 3rd house for a description of what's closest to the client in time and space. The cards in the 4th, 5th, and 6th houses explain more about the client's personal life, domestic conditions, and work situation. The third quadrant cards in the 7th, 8th, and 9th house positions show what the client is actively dealing with in relationships and inter-personal dynamics, as well as what is being planned for the future. The fourth quadrant cards in the 10th, 11th, and 12th house positions give indications of outcomes from the other three quadrants, as well as what the client may meet in the world in the coming forecast period.

Start to integrate the spread by observing the upper and lower hemispheres to see if there are cards of the same suit, cards that share numbers, same-suit Court cards, and the locations of any Major Arcana cards in the spread. Major Arcana cards exert emphasis to the quadrant and house occupied. Analyze the spread for cards that share the astrological attributions of the Major Arcana card, and if they're harmonious or troublesome cards. Related cards show how the client is processing the forces and multiple layers of meaning embedded in the Major Arcana card.

The final five cover cards are a summation. They, too, may indicate topical themes by element, suit, and number shared with cards already in the spread. If the tarotist waits to place these cards until the central spread has been interpreted, the cover cards can be used to answer a client's specific questions. As a further option, the tarotist can fan the remaining cards on the table and allow the client to draw the final five cover cards.

CHAPTER 7

THE VALA CROSS SPREAD

Now that you've been pounded into submission with the 18-card expanded spiral spread, let's throttle back and explore a spread that does the same job with fewer cards.

The Vala Cross spread (my very own invention) compresses the 12-house spread. The arrangement begins with a modified Cosmic Cross. The 1st house includes cards 1 and 2. The Ascendant pivot is doubled, giving more information about the client's present and recent past. The 7th house includes cards 4 and 5, so there's more about personal relationships and interactions, and the near future. The suceedent and cadent houses are compressed into a single card that represents two houses.

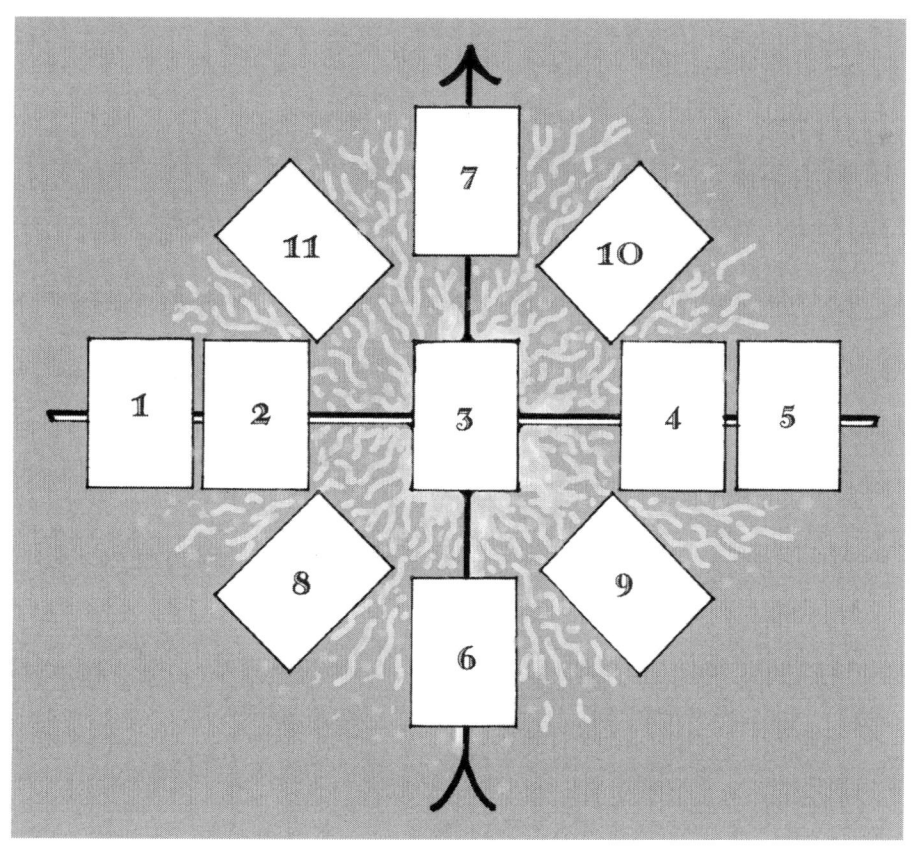

VALA CROSS POSITION MEANINGS

Cards 1 – 2: Ascendant or Self. Personal matters in the recent past, subjects of concern; mental-emotional state in the present.

Card 3: Center. Moderator and filter. Central issues, current situation, emotions, attitudes and focus of the inquiry. May show a person of high importance in the client's life.

Cards 4 – 5: Descendant or Other(s). Relationships, interactions, exchanges, people in the client's life that are of current or near future importance.

Card 6: Nadir or Foundation. The past, foundation, roots of the matter, family, domestic situation, inner life, property matters.

Card 7: Midheaven or Life Path. What will come in the future, choices that are being made, prospects and possibilities. People in authority, people in a prominent position in the client's life, important events and trends in the near future.

Card 8: 2nd and 3rd houses. Personal Assets, resources and activities. Money, possessions, and income-producing skills. Daily activities, regular schedule, people seen on a daily basis; may also include siblings.

Card 9: 5th and 6th houses. Romantic relationships, children, creativity, physical condition, daily efforts and processes in motion. Describes what's being created, worked out, and developed; people and activities of intense interest to the client. High personal and emotional investment zone.

Card 10: 8th and 9th houses. Shared resources, other people's money and transitions. Long-distance and long-term concerns. Educational and spiritual activities. Exchanges with others that benefit or hinder the client.

Card 11: 11th and 12th houses. Outcomes and results. Social networks, people of interest in the outer world, events, plans, hopes for the future. May also relate to situations around children and friends. A difficult card will lean toward 12th house matters like illness, harm, and losses.

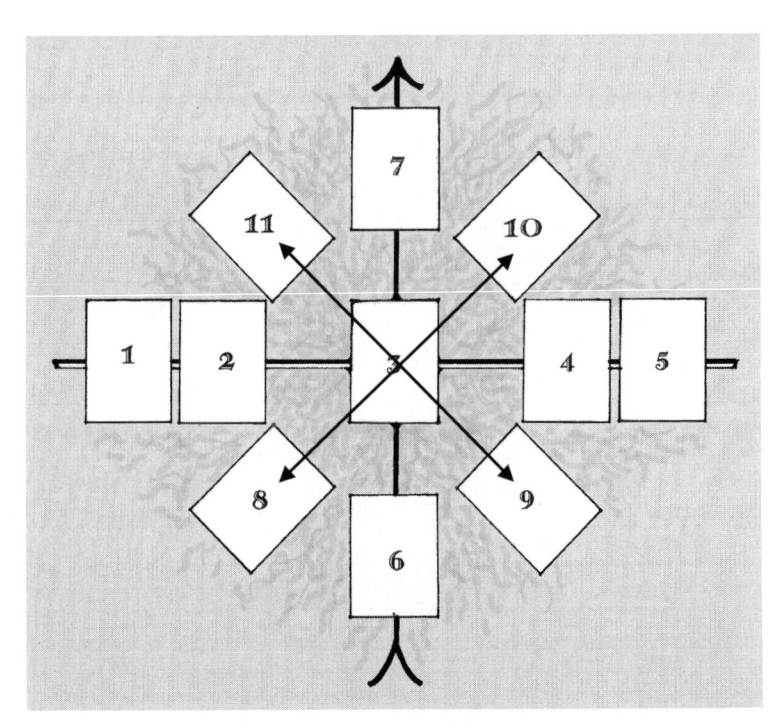

Leveraging the polarities and squares makes the house compression work. The emphasis of this spread is on the Ascendant-Descendant axis. Adding cards to the 1st and 7th houses extends the horizon of encounters. This is an especially good spread for readings about relationships, which seems to be a common concern amongst clients. Additional information about relationships is found in cards 9 and 11.

The central card [3] is the moderator-axle that filters the spread's polarities. Pay attention to the cross-quarter axes cards—they can "see" one another across the axis (Cards 8-10 and 9-11).

Energy from the bottom hemisphere rises up to the cards in the upper hemisphere through the diagonal axes. These axes contain information about the present and future.

Read the bottom three cards as a sequence that describes the inner life and intimate situations (cards 8 – 6 – 9). Read the top three cards as a sequence that describes results, outcomes, and the future (cards 10 – 7 – 11).

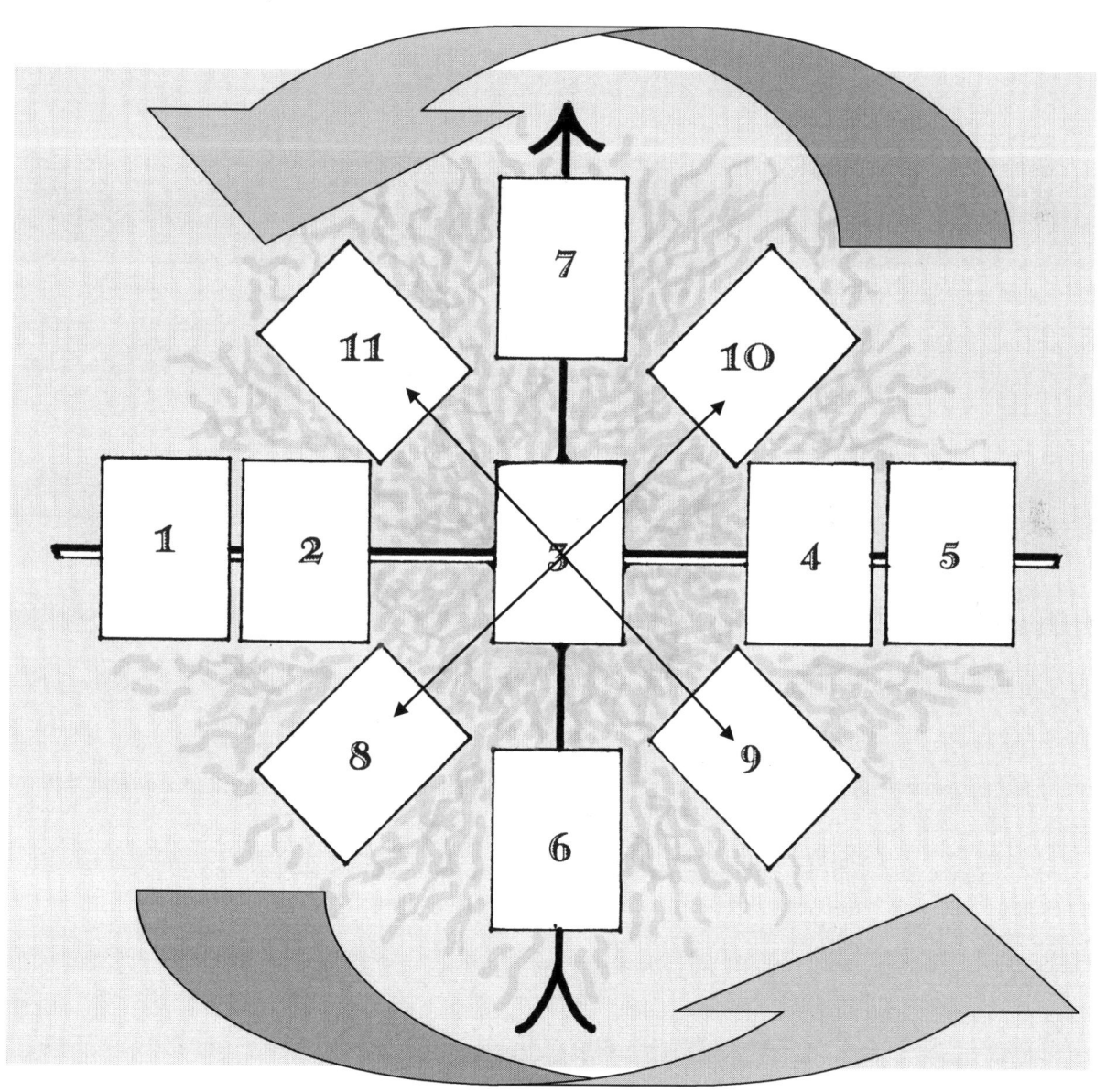

The illustration of this spread presented in **Tarot Decoded** shows two cards in the central position of this spread, resulting in six cards across the horizon. Over the years I've modified the spread and found that a single central card works well.

This spread may be expanded with final axis cover cards. The final 16th card covers the central (3) card.

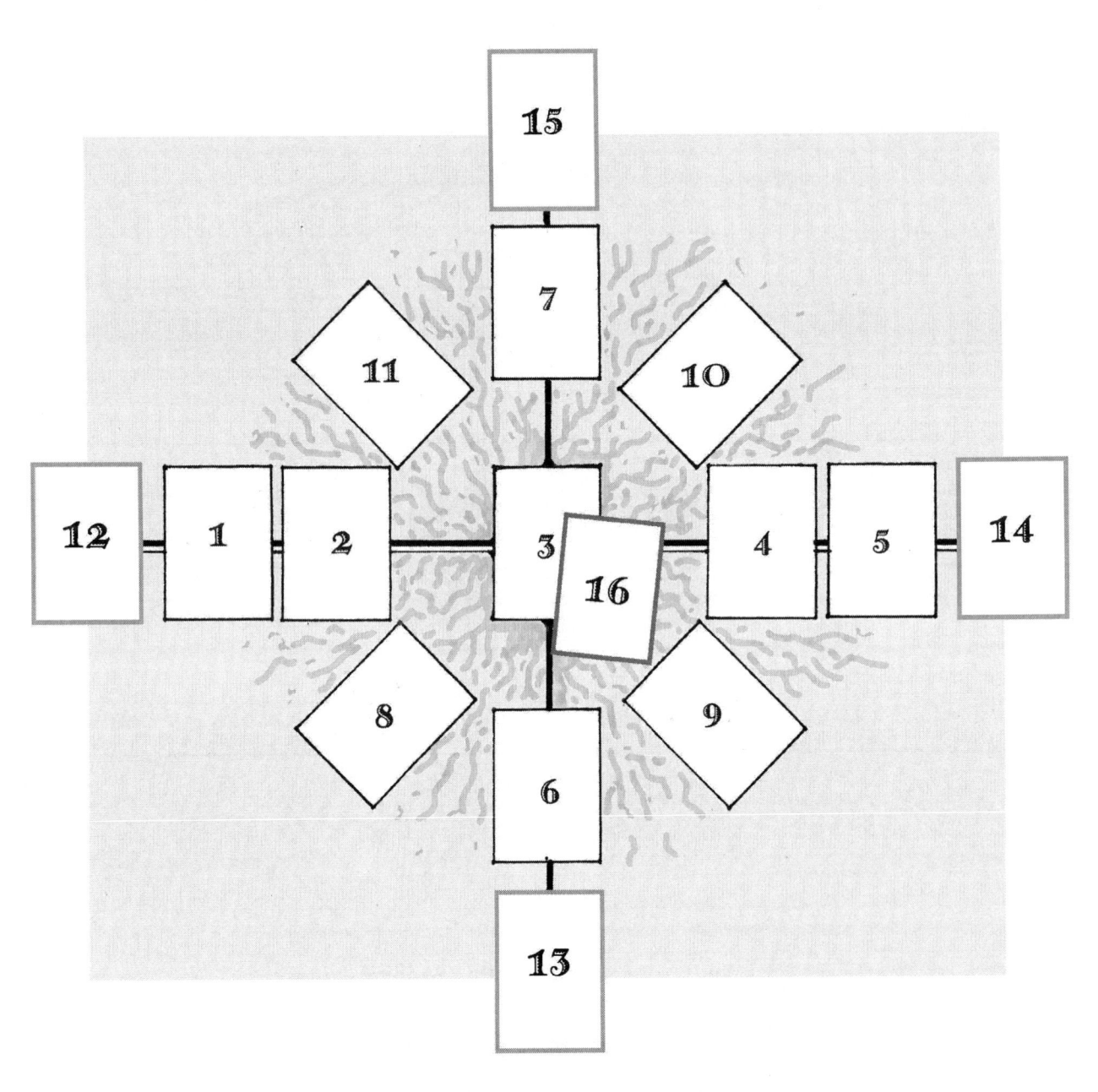

Expanded Vala Cross Spread

Some readers may wonder if I actually place the cards at an angle as shown in the diagram. The answer is: yes, I do. Placing this way emphasizes the relationship with the other angled cards. It makes the circular nature of the spiral arrangement more prominent, and it looks more interesting on the table.

If it seems odd, try it a few times to see if you like it. It's always worked well for me, but everyone has their own preferences and reading styles. Diversity adds to the beauty of the world. Your cards, your reading, your choice. Always.

The High Priestess by E. M. Hazel
August 2017

CHAPTER 8

THE EXPANDED COSMIC CROSS SPREAD

This form shares the shape and spread pattern of the Vala Cross with fewer cards. The two useful cross-quarter (diagonal) axes are added. Both the Vala Cross and the expanded Cosmic Cross are easier and quicker to read than full 12-house arrangements. They can be used when reading time is more limited at psychic fairs and for short consultations.

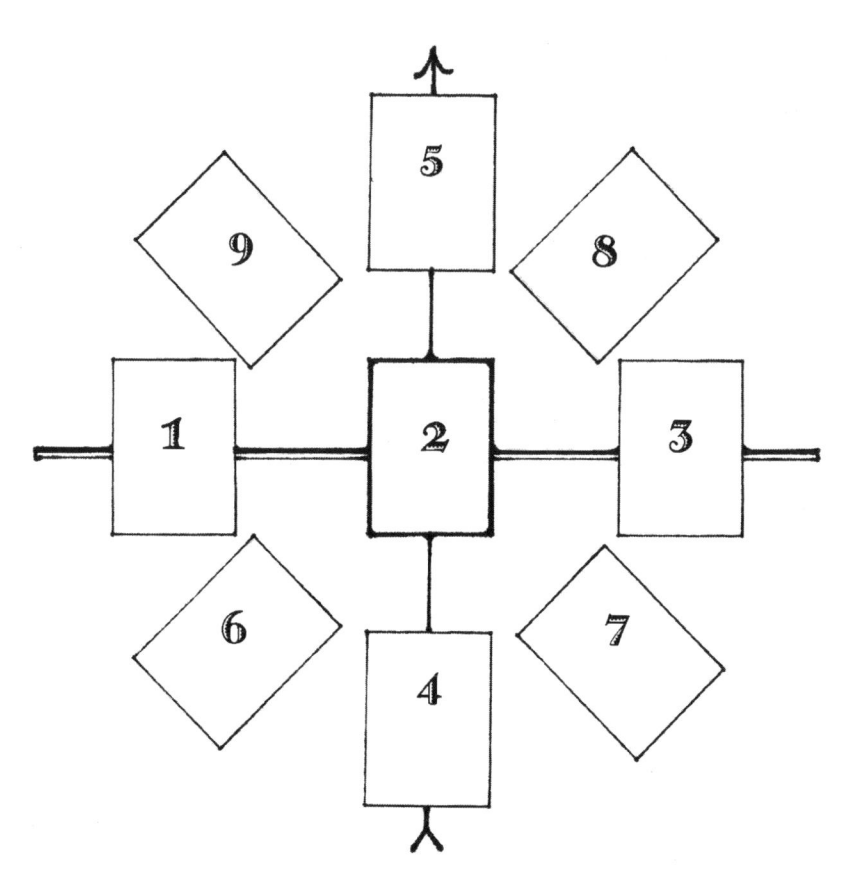

The position meanings are identical to those of the Vala Cross. The only difference is that one card instead of two occupies the Ascendant and Descendant positions. The spread begins with the Cosmic Cross as shown in Chapter 2, then continues with one more spiral of cards into cross-quarter (diagonal) positions.

62   Twelve-House Tarot Spreads

Options for expanding the spread include a final cover card on the center position.

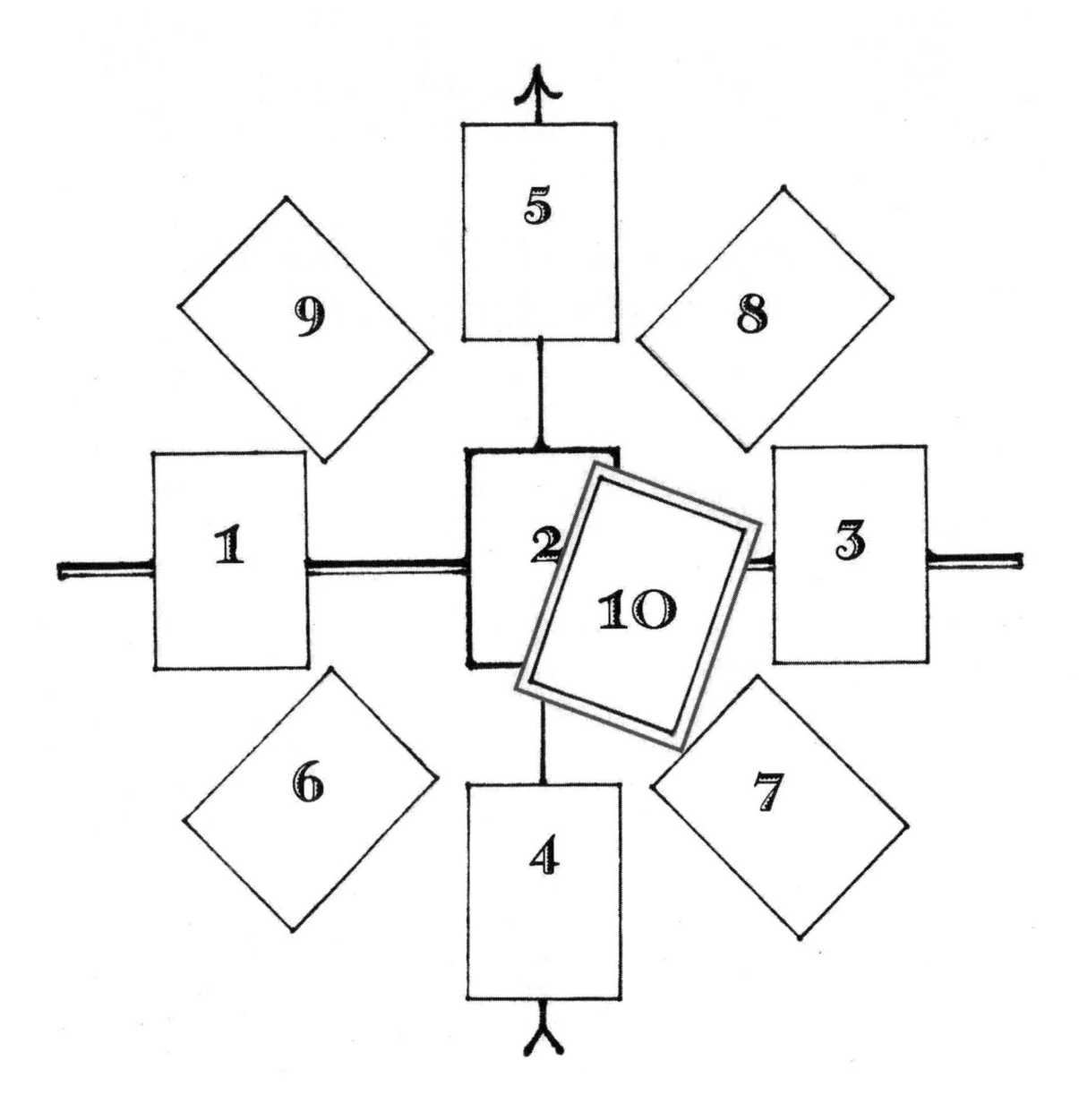

The Expanded Cosmic Cross Spread   63

If you wish, a full outer spiral can be added with a final center card.

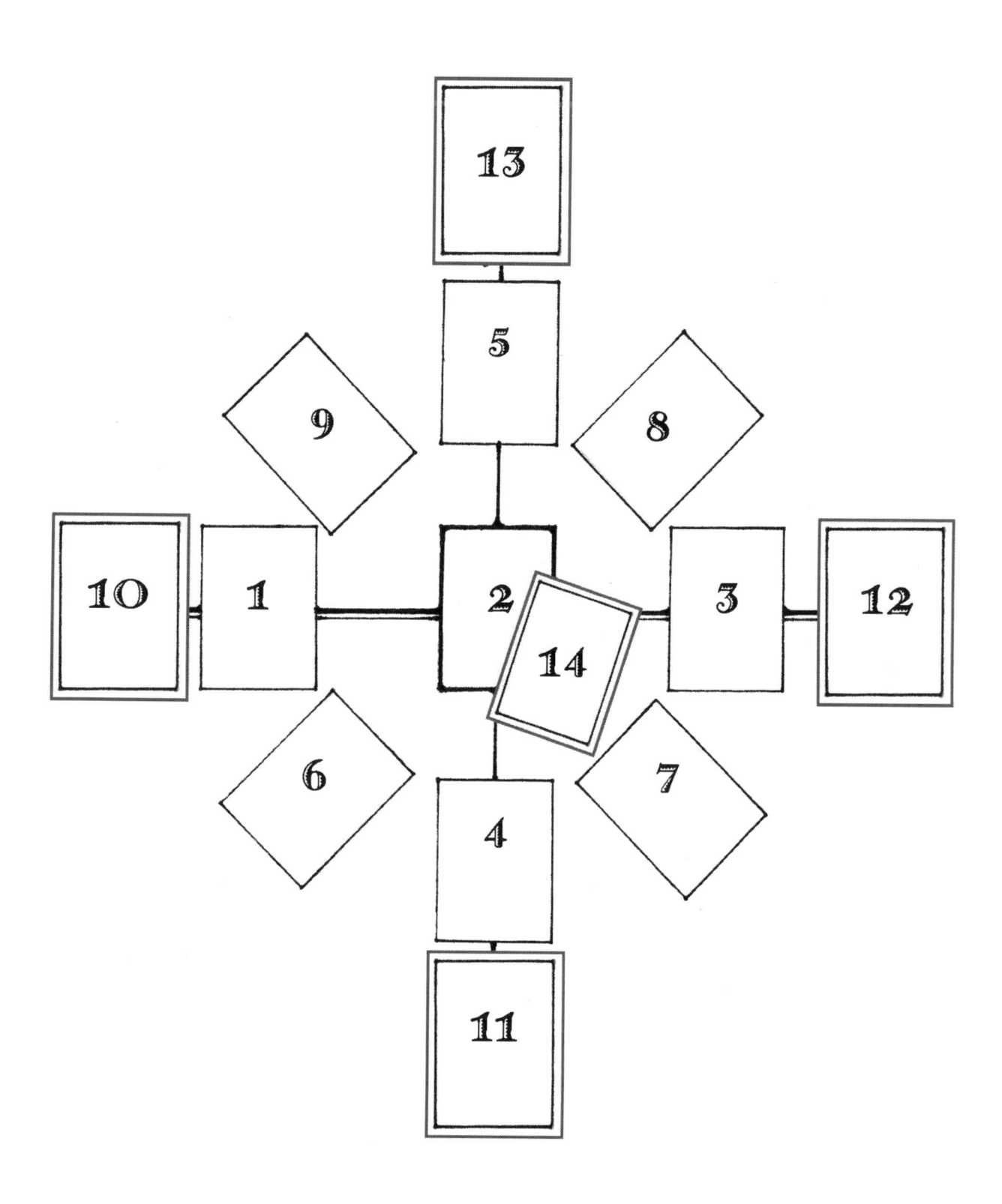

The basic spread is nine cards. A single central cover card produces a ten-card spread. If cards are placed on the pivots and center, it becomes a fourteen-card spread. The reader can control the size of the spread to suit personal preferences and the time available for the reading.

END WITH A FLOURISH

Integrate a separate Major Arcana-only deck at the end of the reading. After the main points of the spread have been interpreted, fan a 22-card Majors-only deck in front of the client and ask him or her to choose one final card. It can be placed in the center of the reading as a final comprehensive indicator. Major Arcana cards are thematic and show over-arching trends and patterns in a client's life. A final Major Arcana card points to significant influences that could supercede other considerations in life. This technique can be used with any spread. Clients enjoy the extra interaction with another deck of cards.

To make this process even more playful, shuffle the Majors-only deck and have the client cut and re-stack it. Offer the client two dice and have her shake and cast them. Determine the total on the dice. If the client rolls an eight, take seven cards off the top of the Majors deck, and use the eighth card as the central cover card. The Major Arcana-only deck and dice finale can be used with any spread.

EIGHT-FOLD PATH (SABBATS) SPREAD

This "eight-house" wheel echoes the eight-fold path, the pagan year and its eight sabbats. This spread can be used like the sequential twelve-house/12-month spread. Each card equates with a sabbat. This spread can be performed at Samhain, the Wiccan New Year on October 31.

Another option is to use this spread at Imbolc on February 2. This sabbat usually coincides with the Asian lunar New Year that takes place at the new moon in Aquarius. Be eclectic and mix-and-match these holidays. Combine a tea ceremony with divination.

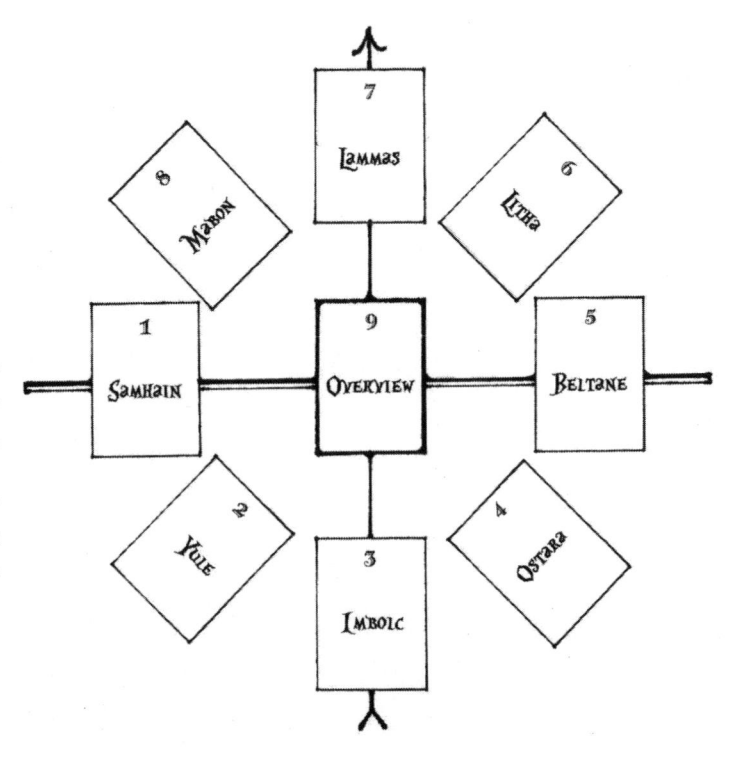

Set up candles, a statue of Buddha or Quan Yin, and brew a pot of Lapsang Soochong tea. Play some east-west fusion music. Perform this spread and complete the reading by casting the I-Ching oracle. Crack open a fortune cookie and play the numbers on the lottery for good luck all year long.

The most cosmically-correct pagan variation places Yule on the Ascendant. In pagan lore, the Sun is reborn on Winter Solstice. The Sun rising equates with sunrise in the east. It's a symbolic Ascendant for the Earth. Performing this spread on sabbats synchronizes personal cycles with the Earth's cycles.

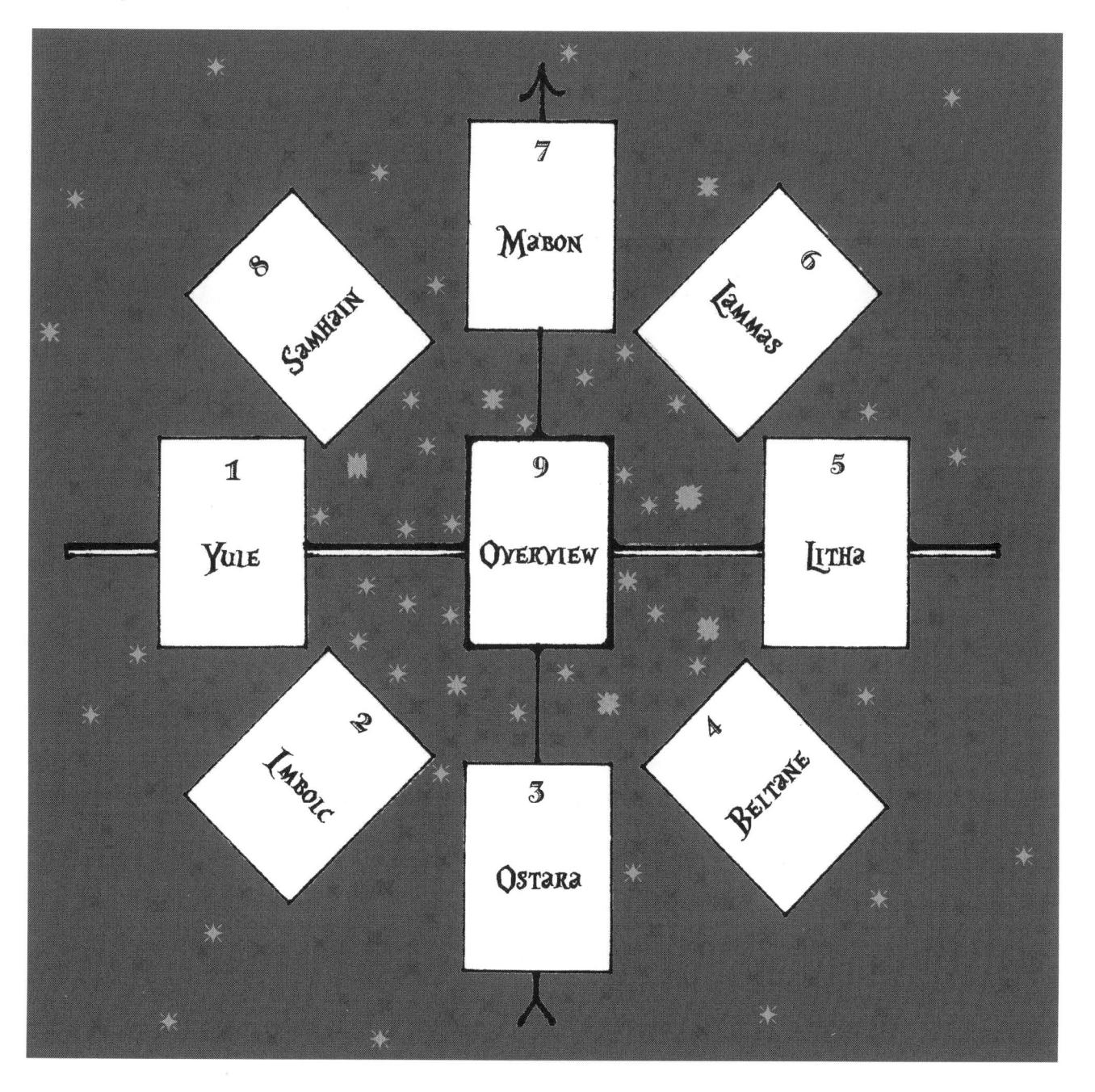

CHAPTER 9

THE ETTEILLA TWELVE-HOUSE SPREAD

Jean-Baptiste Alliette, better known to tarotists as Etteilla (his last name spelled backwards) created the first specifically occult tarot deck: *Grand Etteilla: Ou Tarots Égyptiens* [*Grand Etteilla: Or Egyptian Tarot*]. The Grimaud 1975 edition of the deck is based on Etteilla's original deck published in 1788.

Etteilla also developed the original twelve-house spread. It was described in *Manière de se récréer avec le jeu de cartes nomées tarots* [*How to Have Fun With the Deck of Cards Called Tarot*] published by Segault & Legras in 1785. The spread and technique have been abandoned by tarotists because it relies heavily on astrological techniques. It's a useful and ingenious spread for answering specific questions.

The astrological method underlying this spread is called **horary astrology**. Horary astrology is a rule-bound method for answering specific questions. A chart is erected for the moment that the astrologer understands the client's question. As with tarot, the way a question is phrased is important to the interpretation process. The reader may have to clarify precisely what is being sought through the client's inquiry. Once the chart is erected, it is interpreted by the rules of horary astrology. There are astrologers who specialize in this method.

Etteilla must have worked with a generic tarot deck while developing this spread, since the description of the method given in 1785 predates the occult tarot deck he published in 1788. Perhaps he wrote astrological glyphs on the deck he used. French occultists were experimenting with divinatory methods. Although astrology was in decline, the methods were still sound. Etteilla's twelve-house spread was an ingenious amalgamation. It allowed him to bypass the process of erecting a horary chart by hand while still retaining the ability to answer a client's question. But make no mistake – this is a down-and-dirty shortcut for the horary method! Using a tarot deck rather than an astrological chart forcibly eliminates some of the rules by which a chart is judged.

Clients may ask yes-no questions or questions that elicit more in-depth information. Best results come from questions that are very important and personal to the client: *where is my wedding ring? Will I get the job? Will I get pregnant? Will I win the lawsuit?* Results from horary charts are much less impressive for questions that don't relate directly to the client, like predicting the outcomes of football games and political elections.

Professional horary astrologers always keep records of their consultations, answers, and client outcomes. If an inquiry isn't resolved as predicted, the astrologer returns to the chart to find the interpretive glitch. A collection of horary charts is a teaching and learning tool.

Tarotists who want to experiment with Etteilla's twelve-house method should emulate this practice and keep a written record of the reading. A printable worksheet for this spread is included with other spreads at the back of the book. The steps for interpretation make it necessary to copy the spread on paper. Write the client's name and the current date at the top. Include the time if you wish.

The steps for performing this spread are summarized at the end of this section. The steps are also on the printable form for this spread.

Step 1: Before starting the procedure, go through the tarot deck and remove the twelve Major Arcana cards attributed to the zodiac signs. Zodiacal attributions from the Etteilla, Wirth and Golden Dawn systems are below:

	Etteilla	**Wirth**	**Golden Dawn**
Aries	Hierophant*	Hierophant**	Emperor
Taurus	Sun	Magician	Hierophant
Gemini	Moon	Sun	Lovers
Cancer	Star	Moon	Chariot
Leo	World	Strength	Strength
Virgo	Empress	Empress	Hermit
Libra	Emperor	Justice	Justice
Scorpio	High Priestess	Tower	Death
Sagittarius	Justice	Lovers	Temperance
Capricorn	Temperance	Wheel	Devil
Aquarius	Strength	Temperance	Star
Pisces	Hanged Man	Star	Moon

* *The First Systematic Integration of Tarot and Astrology: Etteilla's Correspondences and Divinatory Method* by Elizabeth Hazel and James Revak. *The Tarot Journal*, Volume II #1, Spring 2002.
** **Tarot of the Magicians** by Oswald Wirth, 1927; new edition with intro by Mary Greer, Weiser 2012, p 40.

As you may notice, there are points of similarity and divergence in these attribution lists. Occultists will argue about anything!

Step 2: The twelve zodiac cards are used to form a 12-house arrangement before the rest of the deck is shuffled. The card for the *current sun sign* is placed in the first house. Arrange the remaining cards in zodiacal sequence through the houses. Gather the remaining cards in a pile.

Using the current sun sign for the first house provides planetary rulers for all twelve houses. With Pisces (The Moon or Eclipse card) in the first house, the ruler of the first house is Jupiter. This planet automatically signifies the querent or client, too.

Example below: On February 23, 2021, the Sun is in Pisces. The tarot card assigned to Pisces in the Golden Dawn attributions occupies the first house, followed by the card for Aries, etc.

When question was asked, the Sun was in Pisces.

The card in the 1st House position is the Moon card, attributed to Pisces.

Step 3: The client must ask a question. The reader must understand the question. For instance, the question "*Where is my missing cat?*" is different from "*Will I find my missing cat?*" The first question makes the cat's location the object of the spread. The second question asks if the inquirer will find the cat, a yes-no question. Both questions can be answered by improving the question to "*Where can I find my missing cat?*" The reader may have to assist the client in selecting the precise phrasing of a question that will elicit the most useful information from the spread.

After the question has been clearly stated, write the question down on the chart form. The client must concentrate on the question while shuffling or cutting the deck.

Step 4: Once the deck has been returned to the reader, the cards are laid out sequentially in house order starting with the first house. The cards are placed face-down around the zodiac circle counter-clockwise. Deal cards into the houses until all the cards have been distributed.

Step 5: The reader must locate the Pentacle pip cards, Ace through Ten. Sort through the stack of cards in each house. All other cards can be restacked and placed face-down in the house position. Return the Pentacle pip cards, face-up, to top of the house pile. ***The house locations of the Pentacle cards must be kept intact.***

Etteilla assigned planetary attributions to the Pentacle (Coins, Deniers) pip cards:

Ace of Pentacles	Sun ☉
Two of Pentacles	Mercury ☿
Three of Pentacles	Venus ♀
Four of Pentacles	Moon ☽
Five of Pentacles	Mars ♂
Six of Pentacles	Jupiter ♃
Seven of Pentacles	Saturn ♄
Eight of Pentacles	North Node ☊
Nine of Pentacles	South Node ☋
Ten of Pentacles	Part of Fortune ⊗

Step 6: Write down the twelve zodiac signs around the chart form on the worksheet. Write the Pentacle pip cards and planet names (or glyphs) in the houses where the cards were found. The result should look something like an astrological chart (a sample spread is given on the following pages).

Step 7: Find the planet(s) that signifies the querent. There are only three planets sought in the spread: the two planetary significators of the **querent** (*client*); and the planetary significator of the **quesited** (*the object sought, the answer to the question*).

The primary significator of the querent is always the planetary ruler of the first house. The querent's co-significator is always the Moon. The current sun-sign card in the 1st house provides the primary significator: the planet that rules the current sun sign.

Aries – Mars **Leo – Sun** **Sagittarius – Jupiter**	**Taurus – Venus** **Virgo – Mercury** **Capricorn – Saturn**	**Gemini – Mercury** **Libra – Venus** **Aquarius – Saturn**	**Cancer – Moon** **Scorpio – Mars** **Pisces – Jupiter**

The sign rulers given above are the ancient planetary rulers. There are no outer planets included in Etteilla's attributions to the Pentacle pip cards. He developed his method before Uranus, Neptune, and Pluto were discovered. The invisible outer planets aren't necessary to interpret the spread.

Example: If this spread is used to answer a question on July 28th, the first house sun-sign is Leo. Leo is ruled by the Sun. In a spread with this sign in the first house, the planetary significators for the querent are the Sun and Moon.

Step 8: Identify is the planetary significator of the quesited. The planet that rules the house of the quesited object supplies the answer to the question. If the question is about marriage, a spouse, or a lawsuit, the planet that rules the sign in the seventh house is the significator. If the question is about a missing pet, the ruler of the sixth house is sought. The answer to "Will I get the job?" is the ruler of the tenth house sign. The ruler of the second house is the significator for a query about the location of a missing personal possession (keys, jewelry, a book, a television remote, etc). Planets are natural object significators; The Sun—gold items; Moon—silver items; Venus—jewelry and clothing, a woman; Mercury—keys, little tools, books, papers, a child; Mars—hot/burning items, iron, sharp objects, tools with motors, a man; Jupiter—religious items; Saturn—antiques, heirlooms, an elderly person. These provide a secondary significator of what's being sought if the primary significator planet of the quesited doesn't answer immediately answer the question.

Step 9: When the planetary significators of the querent and quesited have been identified, look for those planets in the chart-spread. Identify the houses and signs where these significators are located.

Step 10: Determine if there is an aspect relationship between these planets – a sextile, square, trine, opposition, or conjunction (same house). There's no math to fiddle with in this spread form. The planets are in aspect only by house relationship. Don't sweat it—there are some no-brainer tricks for answering questions given below.

EASY WAYS TO MAKE A JUDGMENT

- If both planets are in even-numbered houses, or both in odd-numbered houses, the answer will probably be "yes."

- If one significator planet is in an even-numbered house, and the other is in an odd-numbered house, the answer is probably "no," or the item/person/answer is more challenging to find.

- The answer is more definitively *yes* or *no* if one of the significator planets is in a pivotal house (1st – 4th – 7th – 10th). As always, a significator in a pivot or angular house has a lot of power.

If the planetary significator of the querent makes no connection to the significator of the quesited (i.e., one in an even-numbered and one in an odd-numbered house), then compare the position of the Moon to the significator of the quesited with the same criteria. Check the secondary significators of the quesited and see if this planet can provide more information. Horary spreads tend to be very definitive if the client is in need. Unclear spreads may indicate the client is asking too far in advance, too late, or the question is irrelevant.

Tarot tip: If the Saturn card (7 of Pentacles) is in the 7th house, the spread is a dud, a lemon. It's a signal that the reader can't answer the question. The question is bad or something else is going on (whether the client knows about it or not). The reading won't produce the desired answer. Beware of this placement!

This down-and-dirty horary method is surprisingly effective. Cards can do a good job of answering questions correctly. Any tarotist with a grasp of planet, sign and house meanings can work with this spread. Consider trying it out with a friend or relative who has a pressing personal question. It's a wonderful spread for non-tarot reading horary astrologers to experiment with. Detailed answers require knowledge of astrology and specific information about the rules of horary. That said, good tarotists are often quite intuitive and may do equally well in providing answers.

I have included Etteilla's twelve-house spread in this book because it's historically important. Etteilla was a French occultist and his book has never been fully translated into English. The article "***The First Systematic Integration of Tarot and Astrology: Etteilla's Correspondences and Divinatory Method***" (cited beneath the zodiac/card attribution list) provided the first presentation of his method in the English language. **The Tarot Journal** was a wonderful peer-reviewed, members-only publication published by the International Tarot Society. The article had a somewhat limited circulation at the time, but the article is still posted on the site given in the bibliography. It's important to preserve and pass on information about historic tarot techniques.

SAMPLE SPREAD

This is a photo of an Etteilla-style twelve-house spread. The zodiacal trump were arranged in order, starting with the Hierophant for Taurus. The remaining cards were shuffled and dealt face-down into the houses.

Once dealt, each pile was checked for Pentacle pip cards. These were turned over and returned to the house. In this spread, the 3rd, 6th, 10th, and 12th houses didn't have any Pentacle pip cards—those piles were simply returned face-down.

When the spread was completed, the locations of the Pentacle pip cards were noted in the worksheet (left). You don't have to use colored pens.

The chart produced by this tarot spread is a horary chart, which is interpreted following the rules of horary astrology.

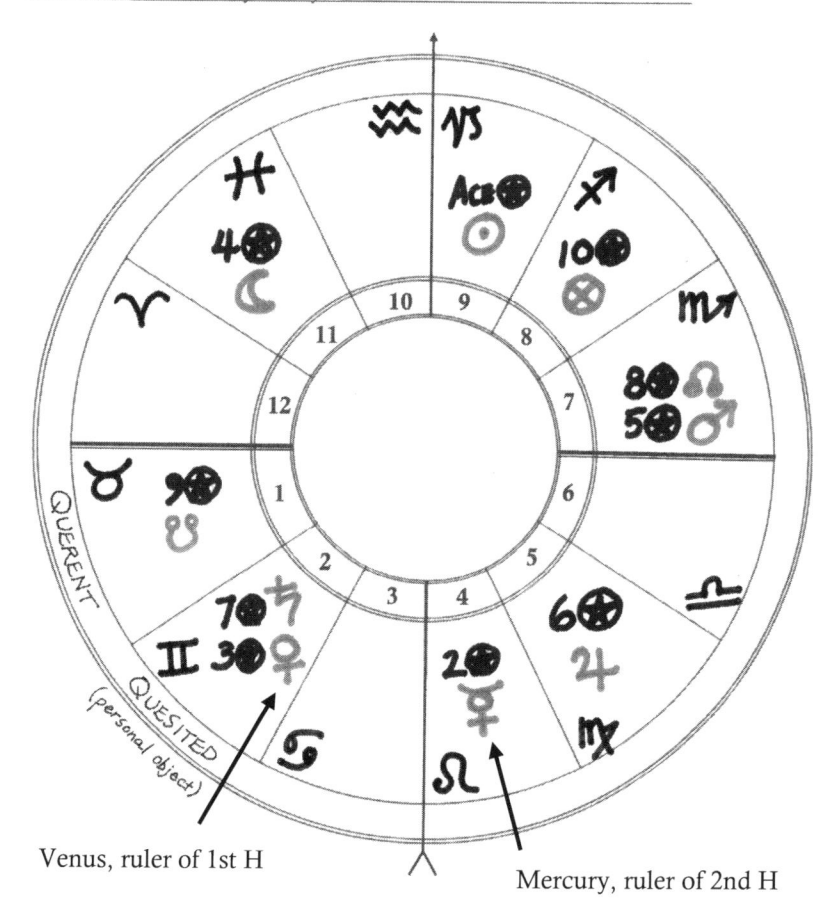

Bob's question: Where are my keys? The Sun was in Taurus on May 10, so the glyph for Taurus was written in the first house, with the other signs following sequentially.

CLIENT NAME: Bob
DATE: May 10, 2014
QUESTION: Where are my car keys?

Venus, ruler of 1st H
Mercury, ruler of 2nd H

Bob's significator is Taurus's ruler **Venus**. The quesited, his keys, are shown by the ruler of the second house **Mercury** (Gemini). Venus is in the 2nd house of personal possessions and sextiles Mercury in the 4th house. The question "Where are my keys?" implicitly asks if Bob will find them. Venus and Mercury, the significators, are both in even-numbered houses, the 2nd and 4th (sextile). The immediate answer is, yes, Bob will find his keys. It's a super-sized YES because Mercury is in a pivotal house.

So where the heck are the keys? Mercury occupies the 4th house, which rules the home. The keys are in Bob's dwelling place. The 4th house is Sun-ruled Leo. The Sun gives light, so the keys are near a sunny window. Since Venus is in the 2nd house, the location of the keys is connected to his personal possessions. Venus rules clothing and jewelry (amongst other things). Bob's keys are probably in a coat or pants pocket. Gemini rules arms and hands, so he should start by looking in his coats. Saturn shares the 2nd house with Venus. Saturn is dark, cold and dry. Bob needs to check the pockets of a coat, not a sweater or hoodie.

Bob found his keys in a coat pocket. The coat was hanging on a hall tree in front of a south-facing window. No kidding!

The spread-chart tells a bit more of the story, although I didn't share this part with Bob. Bob's secondary significator, the Moon, is in Pisces in the 11th house. Pisces Moons are associated with a dreamy state of mind. The Pisces Moon squares Venus and Saturn in Gemini. Bob was in a rush! Saturn rules time, but Gemini never has enough of it. The Moon is in an odd-numbered house and can't "see" Mercury in the 4th house (an inconjunction, an aspect not always used in horary analysis). But Venus can "see" Mercury two houses away, so the keys will be found with ease. The keys were found when Bob cooled his jets and took the Saturn-ruled time to look for them.

Explaining all the rules of horary astrology is beyond the scope of this book. Excellent texts about horary astrology are cited in *Suggested Reading* (page 77) for people who might be interested in learning more about this useful technique. Additional information can be found on websites, although these aren't generally as comprehensive or as well-ordered as the descriptions found in books. Horary authors include numerous sample charts so the reader can see how the answer to the question was determined.

CHAPTER 9: SUMMARY OF THE STEPS FOR AN ETTEILLA-STYLE TWELVE-HOUSE SPREAD

Step 1: Remove the Major Arcana zodiacal cards from the deck. Write the client's name and the current date on the worksheet.

Step 2: Arrange the zodiacal Major Arcana cards into the twelve house circle with the current sun-sign in the first house. The other cards follow sequentially through the houses.

Step 3: The client must ask a question. Write it down on the worksheet. The client shuffles or cuts the deck.

Step 4: The cards are dealt face-down into the houses in sequence, starting with the first house, then second house, third house, etc., until all of the cards are in the spread.

Step 5: Sort through the cards in each house pile to locate the ten Pentacle pip cards. Return the pile to the house with the Pentacle cards face up.

Step 6: Write the zodiac signs into the houses on the worksheet. Write the Pentacle cards and planets into the houses where they are located.

Step 7: Identify the querent's planetary significators: the ruler of the first house and the Moon.

Step 8: Identify the planetary significator of the quesited—the house ruler of the item (or person or personal goal) being sought. Another planet may be a natural significator of the quesited.

Step 9: Find the houses where these significators are located in the chart-spread.

Step 10: Determine if there is an aspect relationship between the querent's significator and the significator of the quesited. Both in an even-numbered house—yes. Both in an odd-numbered house—yes. One in an even, one in an odd-numbered house—no. The answer is more definitive if one of the significators is in a pivot (the angular houses 1—4—7—10).

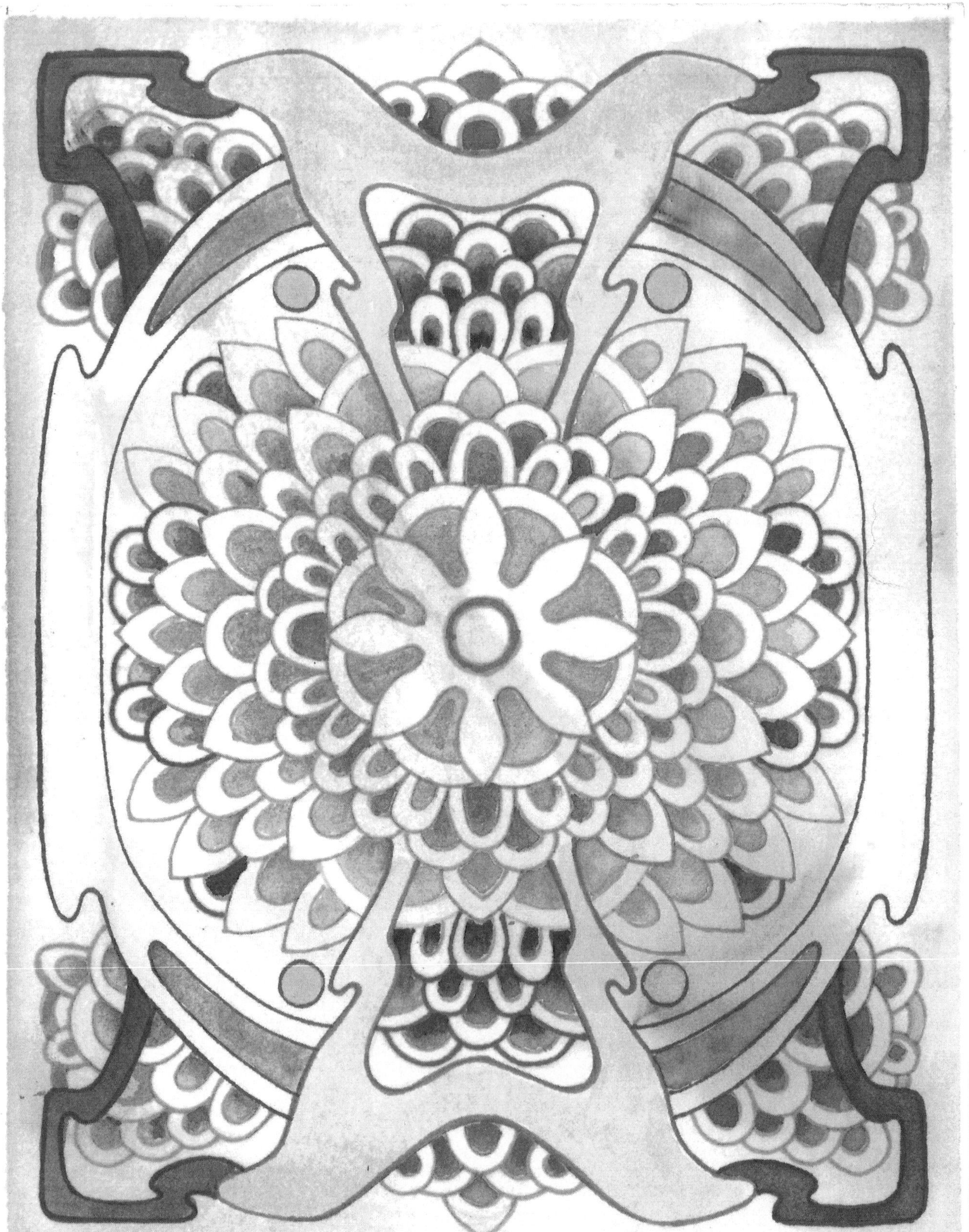

SUGGESTED READING

Astrological Houses

Karen Hamaker-Zondag. *The House Connection: How to Read the Houses in an Astrological Chart.* Weiser, 1994.

Deborah Houlding. *The Houses—Temples of the Sky.* The Wessex Astrologer, 2006.

Bruno and Louise Huber. *The Astrological Houses.* HopeWell, 2011 (Reissue of "Man and His World" 1978)

Howard Sasportas and Liz Greene. *The Twelve Houses.* FLARE, 2010 (revised edition)

Dane Rudhyar. *The Astrological Houses: The Spectrum of Individual Experience.* CRCS Publications, 1986.

Houses from Classical and Medieval Viewpoints

Joseph Crane. *Astrological Roots: The Hellenistic Legacy.* Wessex Astrologer, (Chapter 7—The Twelve Places)

J. Lee Lehman, Ph. D. *Classical Astrology for Modern Living.* Whitford Press.

Jean-Baptiste Morin. *Astrologia Gallica Book Seventeen: The Astrological Houses.* Translated by James Herschel Holden, M.A. AFA, 2008.

Horary Astrology

Barclay, Olivia. *Horary Astrology Rediscovered.* London. Schiffer Publications, Ltd. 1997.

Doane, Doris Chase. *Modern Horary Astrology.* Tempe, AZ. American Federation of Astrologers (no date)

Jones, Marc Edmund. *Horary Astrology: Practical Techniques for Problem Solving.* Aurora Press, 1993. (reprint)

Lewis, James R. *Astrology Encyclopedia.* Detroit, MI. Visible Ink Press (Gale Research, Inc.), 1994.

Louis, Anthony. *Horary Astrology, Plain and Simple.* St. Paul, MN. Llewellyn International, 1998.

English-language works about Etteilla (Jean-Baptiste Alliette)

Elizabeth M. Hazel and James W. Revak. *The First Systematic Integration of Tarot and Astrology: Etteilla's Correspondences and Divinatory Method.* Originally published in *The Tarot Journal*, Vol II, #1,

Spring 2002. See on the web at: http://www.villarevak.org//astro/main.html (This site remains accessible at the time of publication of this text)

Revak, James W. *The Influence of Etteilla and His School on Mathers and Waite*. See on the web at: http://www.villarevak.org//emw/emw_1.htm

Revak, James W., ed. & trans. *Tarot Divination: Three Parallel Traditions*. See on the web at: http://www.villarevak.org//td/td_1.htm

Works by Elizabeth Hazel

Tarot Decoded: Understanding Attributions and Dignities. Weiser, 2004.

The Whispering Tarot deck and *The Whispering Tarot: Softly Spoken Secrets* (accompanying book), Kozmic Kitchen Press, 2008.

APPENDIX
BLANK SPREAD FORMS

The worksheets are provided in the order presented in this book. Spread positions meanings are given for quick reference. I recommend using card abbreviations for filling out the little squares on these forms: W (Wands), Sw (Swords), C (Cups), P or ✪ (Pentacles); P (Page or Princess), Kn (Knight) Q (Queen), K (King); and numbers for the Major Arcana cards. See the sample spread on the following page.

These blank spread forms may be printed for personal use only! Please do not scan copies to post on the web, on Facebook or share to other internet or social media venues. Please do not make copies for distribution or sale, or use for any purpose but private readings for yourself and clients. Tarot educators are asked to contact the author for permission to reproduce for teaching purposes.

You may cut these back pages out of the book to take to a print shop. A copyright permission notice for personal use is on the back of each form. Some print shops will need to see that.

Blank Tarot Spread worksheets

1. The Cosmic Cross Spread—three variations (5 cards)
2. The Sequential Twelve-House Spread—variation 1 (13 cards)
3. The Sequential Twelve-House Spread—variation 2
4. The Sequential Twelve-House Spread—variation 3 (New Year's Spread)
5. The Polarity Twelve-House Spread—variation 1 (13 cards)
6. The Polarity Twelve-House Spread—variation 2
7. The Polarity Twelve-House Spread—variation 3
8. The Spiral Twelve House Spread—variation 1 (13 cards)
9. The Spiral 12-House Spread—variation 2
10. The Spiral 12-House Spread—variation 3 (expanded) (18 cards)
11. The Vala Cross Spread (11 cards)
12. The Vala Cross Spread—expanded (16 cards)
13. The Expanded Cosmic Cross Spread—variation 1 (9 cards)
14. Expanded Cosmic Cross Spread—variation 2 (10 cards)
15. The Expanded Cosmic Cross Spread—variation 3 (14 cards)
16. The Eight-Fold Sabbat Spread (9 cards)
17. The Etteilla Twelve-House Horary Spread (entire deck)

Below is a reduced-size scan of a filled-out spread form. I did a tarot reading few days before this book was released. Things should go very well but there may be some delays (4 Sw).

THE VALA CROSS SPREAD

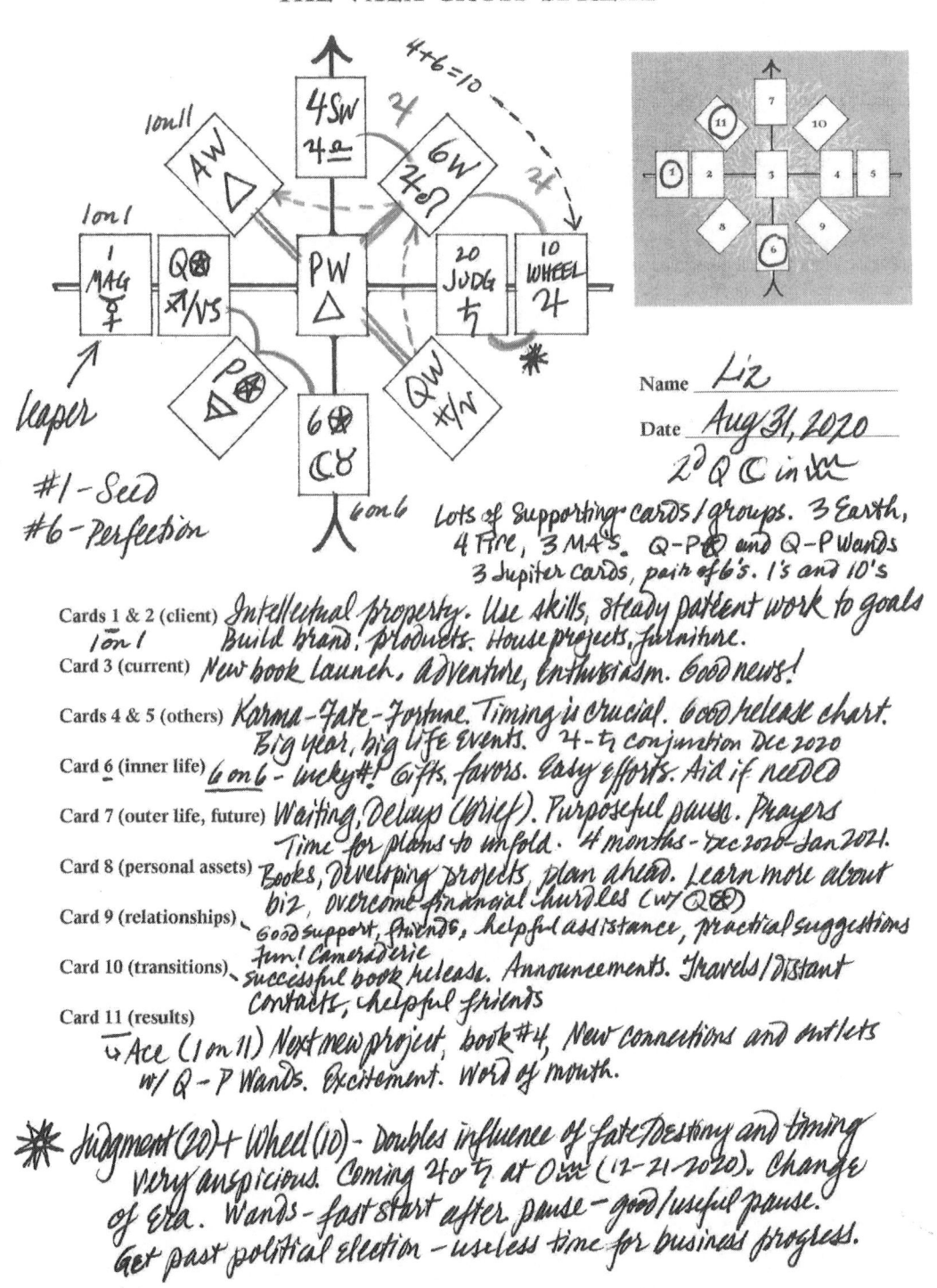

[Handwritten spread diagram with cards placed in cross formation:]

- 4+6=10 (top)
- 4 Sw / 4♎︎ (position 7, top)
- 6 W / 4♌?
- 1 on 11 — A W (position 11)
- 1 on 1 — 1 MAG / ♇ (position 1)
- Q ⊕ / ♐/VS (position 2)
- P W / △ (center, position 3)
- 20 JUDG / ♄ (position 4)
- 10 WHEEL / ♃ (position 5)
- P ⊕ / △ (position 8)
- Q W / ♐/N (position 9)
- 6 ⊕ / C8 (position 6, bottom)
- 6 on 6
- Leaper ↗

#1 — Seed
#6 — Perfection

Name: Liz
Date: Aug 31, 2020
2d Q ☾ in ♏︎

Lots of supporting cards/groups. 3 Earth, 4 Fire, 3 MA's. Q-P⊕ and Q-P Wands. 3 Jupiter cards, pair of 6's. 1's and 10's

Cards 1 & 2 (client): Intellectual property. Use skills, steady patient work to goals. 1 on 1 Build brand, products. House projects, furniture.

Card 3 (current): New book launch. Adventure, Enthusiasm. Good news!

Cards 4 & 5 (others): Karma—Fate—Fortune. Timing is crucial. Good release chart. Big year, big life events. ♃-♄ conjunction Dec 2020

Card 6 (inner life): 6 on 6 — lucky #! Gifts, favors. Easy efforts. Aid if needed

Card 7 (outer life, future): Waiting, Delays (brief). Purposeful pause. Prayers. Time for plans to unfold. 4 months — Dec 2020 – Jan 2021.

Card 8 (personal assets): Books, developing projects, plan ahead. Learn more about biz, overcome financial hurdles (w/ Q⊕)

Card 9 (relationships): Good support, friends, helpful assistance, practical suggestions. Fun! Cameraderie

Card 10 (transitions): successful book release. Announcements. Travels/Distant contacts, helpful friends

Card 11 (results): ↳ Ace (1 on 11) Next new project, book #4, New connections and outlets w/ Q-P Wands. Excitement. Word of mouth.

✳ Judgment (20) + Wheel (10) — Doubles influence of fate/Destiny and timing. Very auspicious. Coming ♃ σ ♄ at 0♒︎ (12-21-2020). Change of Era. Wands — fast start after pause — good/useful pause. Get past political election — useless time for business progress.

THE COSMIC CROSS SPREAD – VARIATIONS 1, 2 AND 3

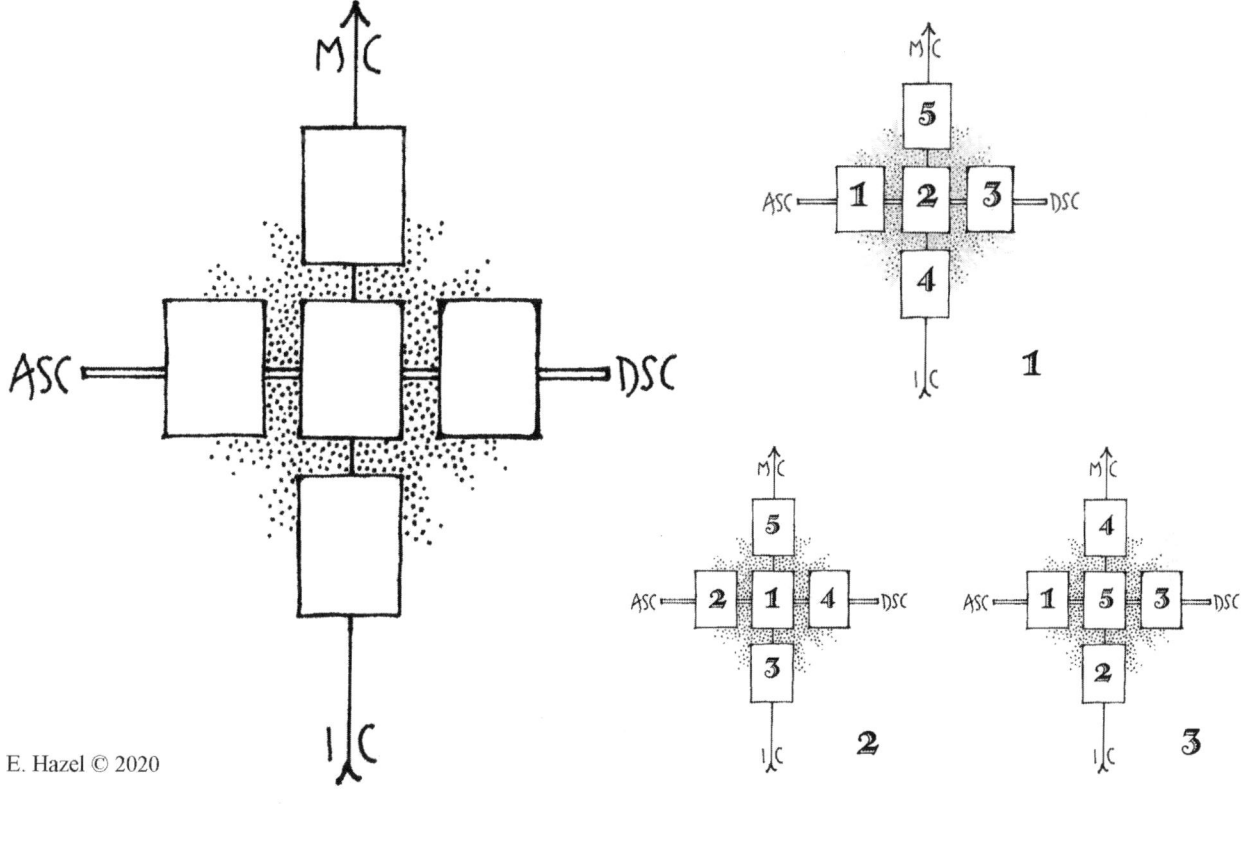

E. Hazel © 2020

Name _____ Date _____

Ascendant Card:

IC Card:

Descendant Card:

MC Card:

Center Card:

Notice to print shops:
The owner of this book has permission to make copies of this blank spread form for personal use only.

These forms are not for resale, nor are they to be scanned or shared on the internet in any form.

Elizabeth Hazel © 2020 Kozmic Kitchen Press
For more information or use for educational purposes contact Liz at
www.kozmickitchenpress.com

THE SEQUENTIAL 12-HOUSE SPREAD — VARIATION 1

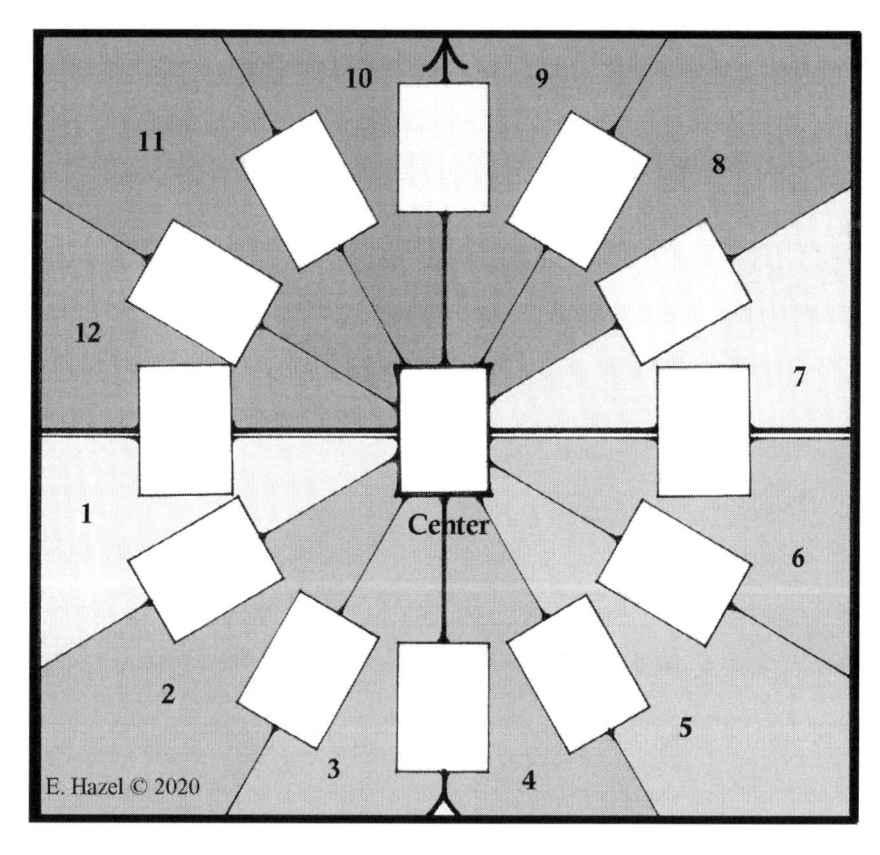

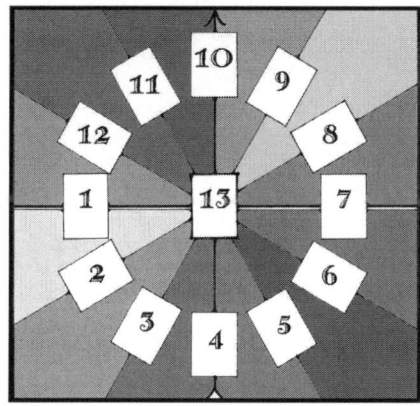

Name

Date

First House (self)

Second House (money)

Third House (movement)

Fourth House (home)

Fifth House (love)

Sixth House (work)

Seventh House (partners)

Eighth House (changes)

Ninth House (self-development)

Tenth House (life-path)

Eleventh House (results)

Twelfth House (hidden issues)

Center

Notice to print shops:
The owner of this book has permission to make copies of this blank spread form for personal use only.

These forms are not for resale, nor are they to be scanned or shared on the internet in any form.

Elizabeth Hazel © 2020 Kozmic Kitchen Press
For more information or use for educational purposes contact Liz at
www.kozmickitchenpress.com

THE SEQUENTIAL 12-HOUSE SPREAD — VARIATION 2

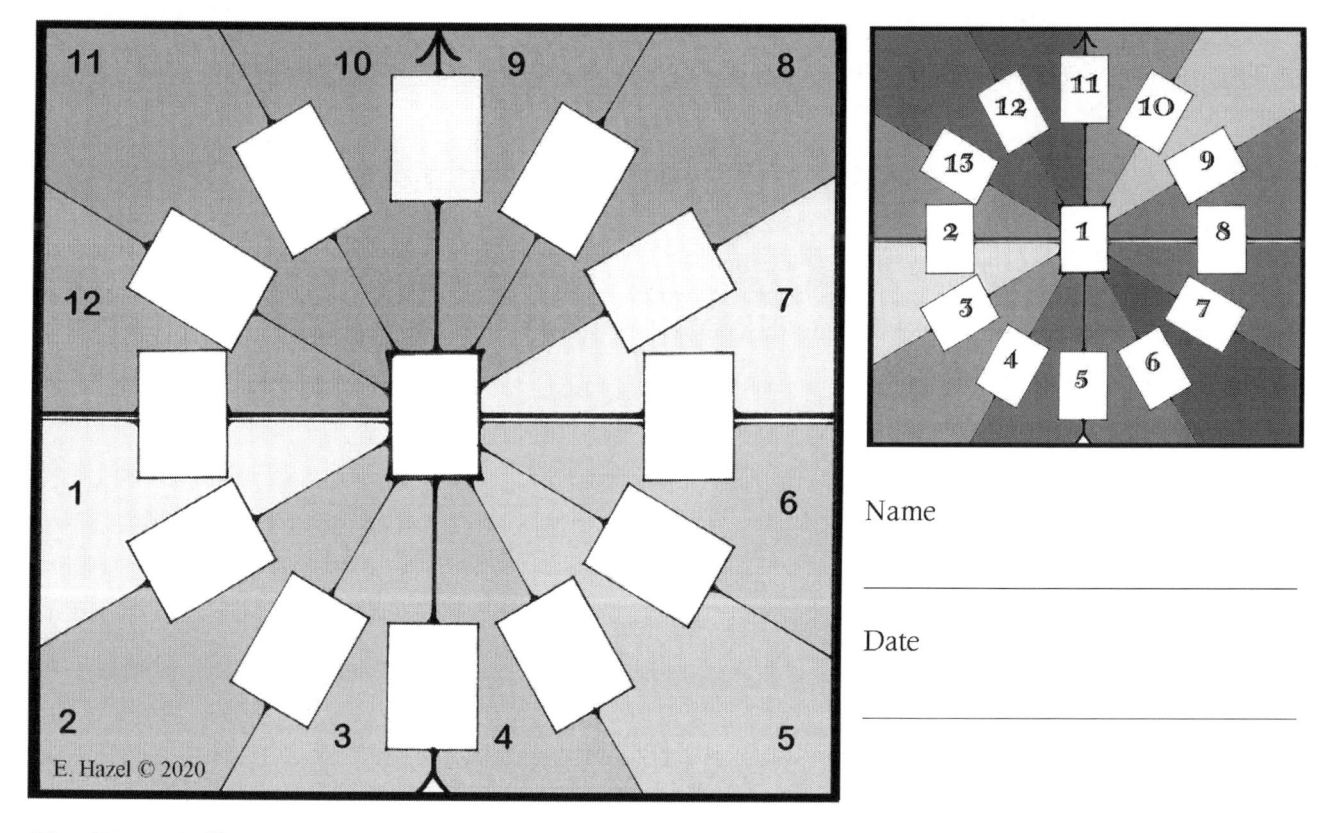

Name

Date

First House (self)

Second House (money)

Third House (movement)

Fourth House (home)

Fifth House (love)

Sixth House (work)

Seventh House (partners)

Eighth House (changes)

Ninth House (self-development)

Tenth House (life-path)

Eleventh House (results)

Twelfth House (hidden issues)

Center

Notice to print shops:
The owner of this book has permission to make copies of this blank spread form for personal use only.

These forms are not for resale, nor are they to be scanned or shared on the internet in any form.

Elizabeth Hazel © 2020 Kozmic Kitchen Press
For more information or use for educational purposes contact Liz at
www.kozmickitchenpress.com

THE SEQUENTIAL 12-HOUSE SPREAD — VARIATION 3

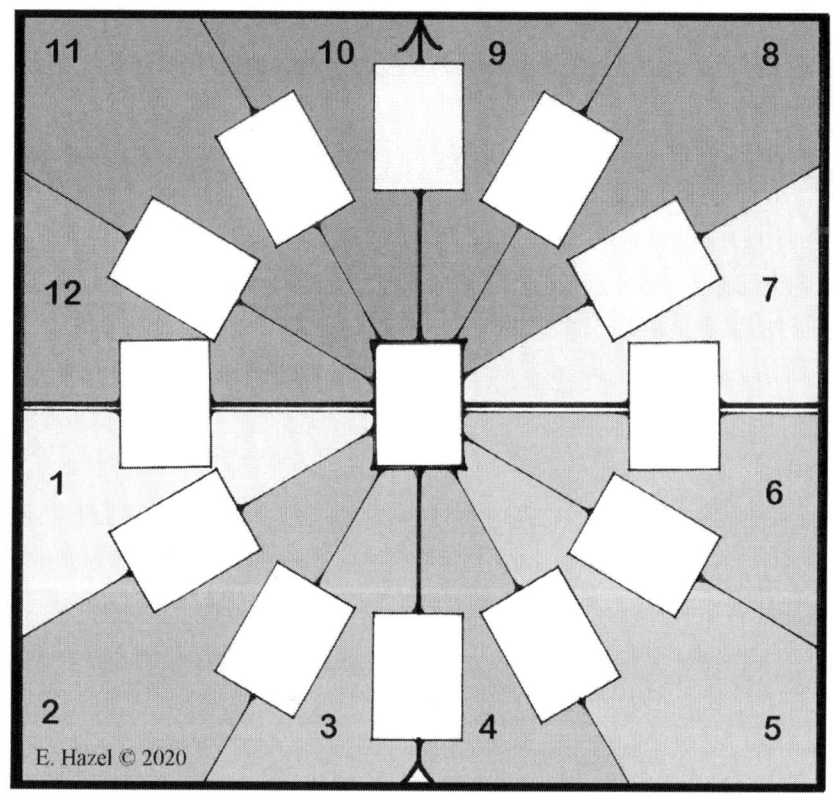

New Year's or 12-Month Spread

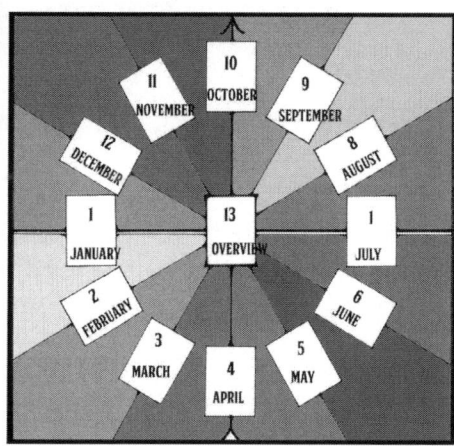

Name

_____

Date

_____

First House (self)

Second House (money)

Third House (movement)

Fourth House (home)

Fifth House (love)

Sixth House (work)

Seventh House (partners)

Eighth House (changes)

Ninth House (self-development)

Tenth House (life-path)

Eleventh House (results)

Twelfth House (hidden issues)

Center

Notice to print shops:
The owner of this book has permission to make copies of this blank spread form for personal use only.

These forms are not for resale, nor are they to be scanned or shared on the internet in any form.

Elizabeth Hazel © 2020 Kozmic Kitchen Press
For more information or use for educational purposes contact Liz at
www.kozmickitchenpress.com

THE POLARITY 12-HOUSE SPREAD — VARIATION 1

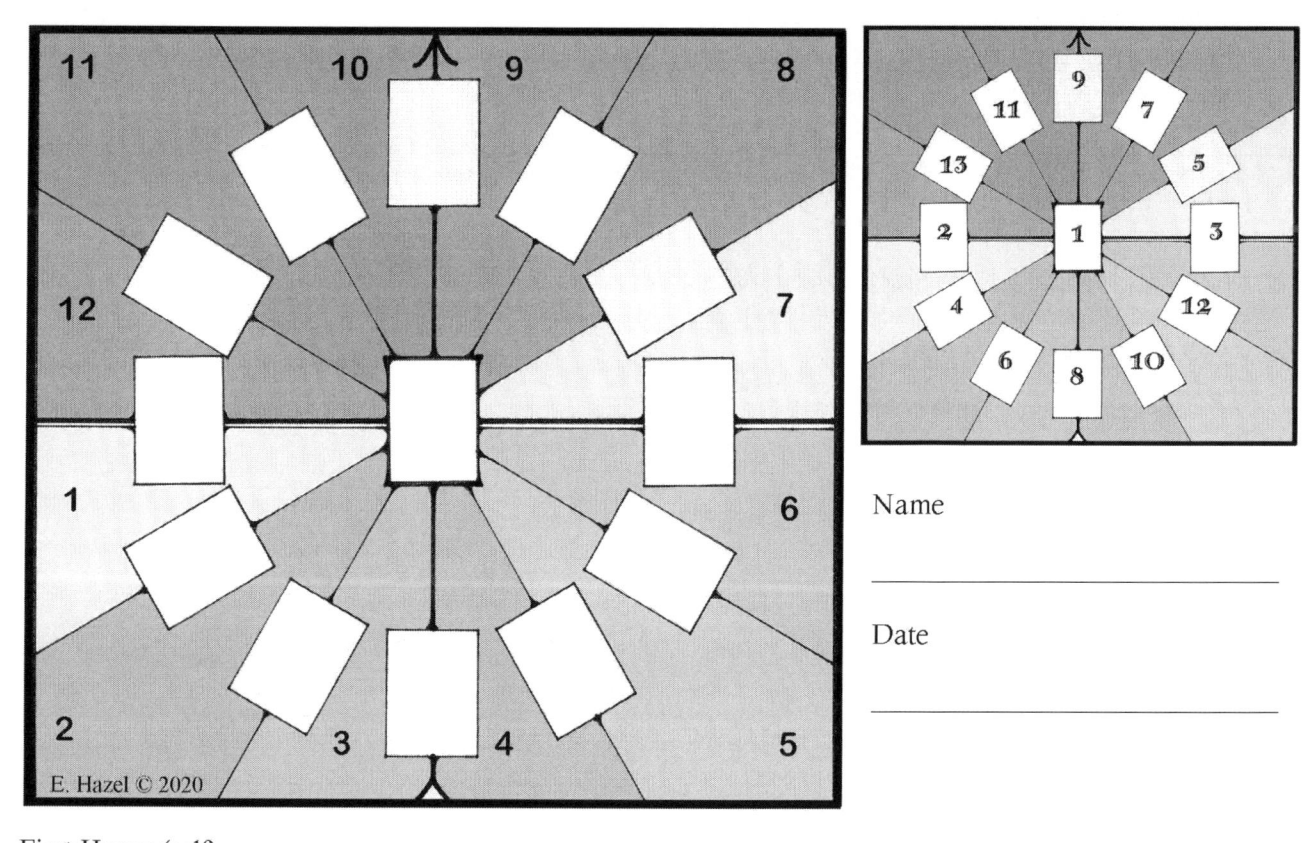

First House (self)

Second House (money)

Third House (movement)

Fourth House (home)

Fifth House (love)

Sixth House (work)

Seventh House (partners)

Eighth House (changes)

Ninth House (self-development)

Tenth House (life-path)

Eleventh House (results)

Twelfth House (hidden issues)

Center

Notice to print shops:
The owner of this book has permission to make copies of this blank spread form for personal use only.

These forms are not for resale, nor are they to be scanned or shared on the internet in any form.

Elizabeth Hazel © 2020 Kozmic Kitchen Press
For more information or use for educational purposes contact Liz at
www.kozmickitchenpress.com

THE POLARITY 12-HOUSE SPREAD — VARIATION 2

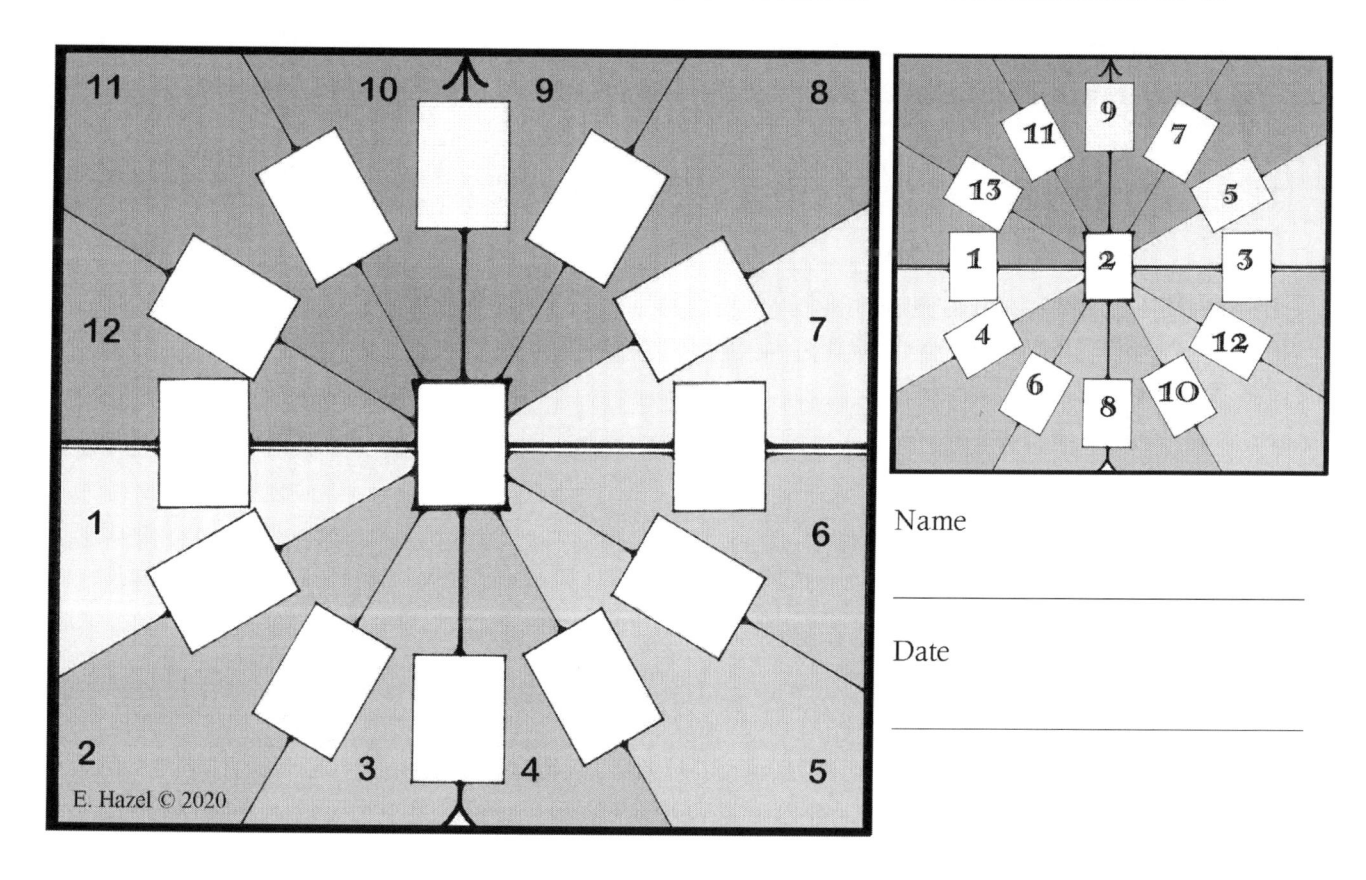

Name

Date

First House (self)

Second House (money)

Third House (movement)

Fourth House (home)

Fifth House (love)

Sixth House (work)

Seventh House (partners)

Eighth House (changes)

Ninth House (self-development)

Tenth House (life-path)

Eleventh House (results)

Twelfth House (hidden issues)

Center

Notice to print shops:
The owner of this book has permission to make copies of this blank spread form for personal use only.

These forms are not for resale, nor are they to be scanned or shared on the internet in any form.

Elizabeth Hazel © 2020 Kozmic Kitchen Press
For more information or use for educational purposes contact Liz at
www.kozmickitchenpress.com

THE POLARITY 12-HOUSE SPREAD — VARIATION 3

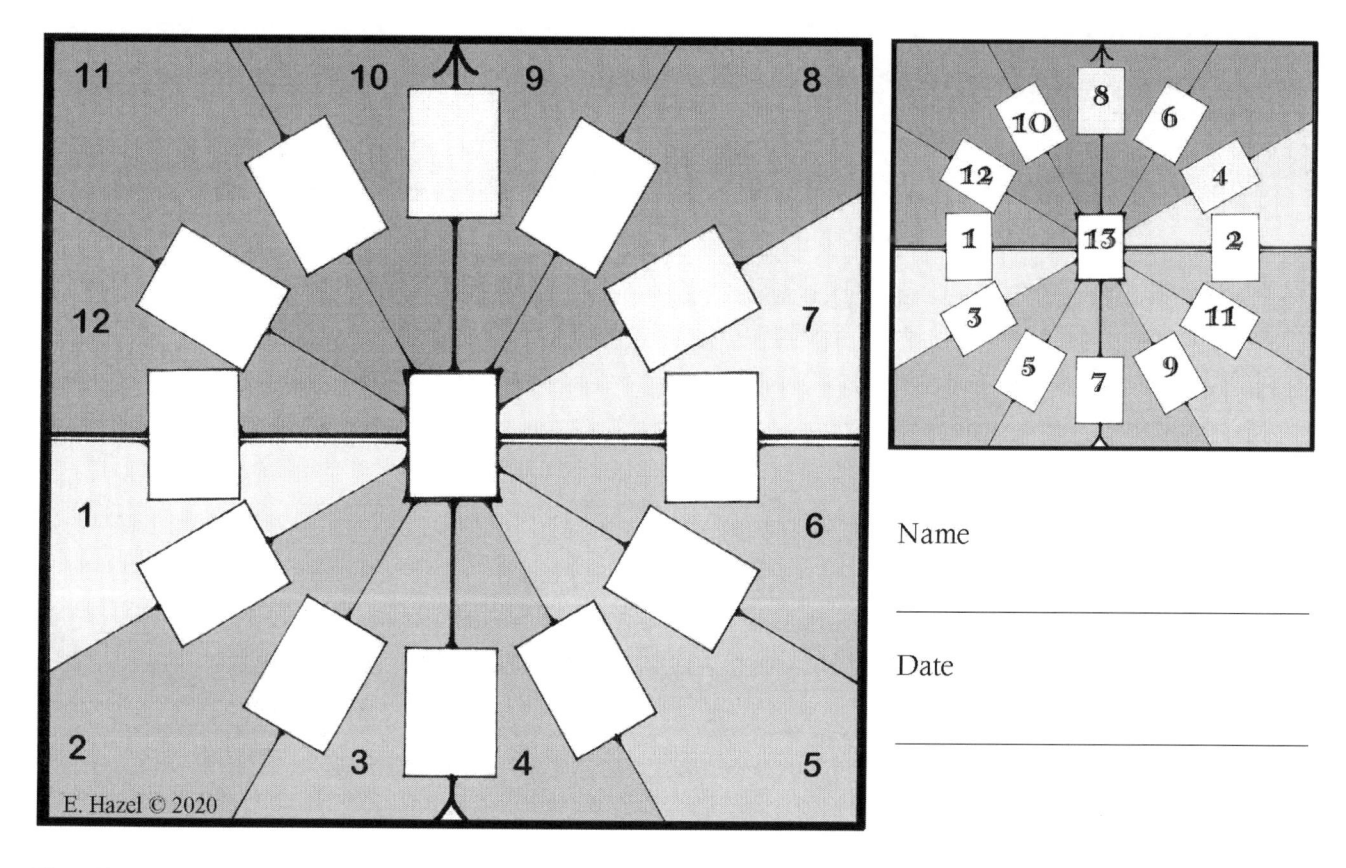

Name

Date

First House (self)

Second House (money)

Third House (movement)

Fourth House (home)

Fifth House (love)

Sixth House (work)

Seventh House (partners)

Eighth House (changes)

Ninth House (self-development)

Tenth House (life-path)

Eleventh House (results)

Twelfth House (hidden issues)

Center

Notice to print shops:
The owner of this book has permission to make copies of this blank spread form for personal use only.

These forms are not for resale, nor are they to be scanned or shared on the internet in any form.

Elizabeth Hazel © 2020 Kozmic Kitchen Press
For more information or use for educational purposes contact Liz at
www.kozmickitchenpress.com

THE SPIRAL 12-HOUSE SPREAD – VARIATION 1

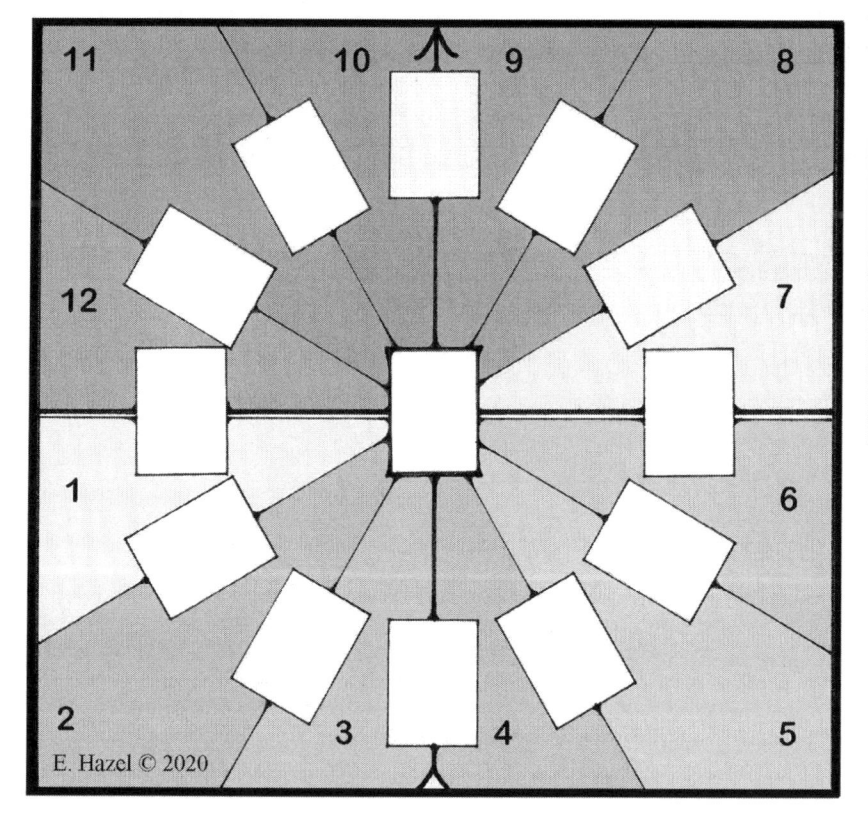

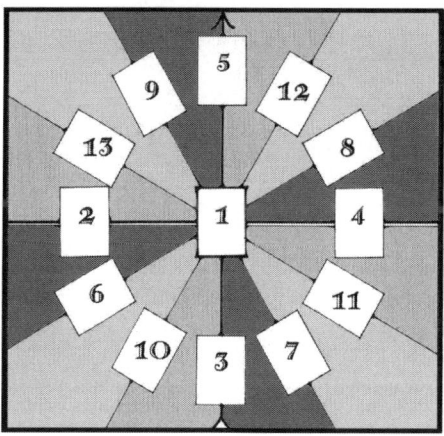

Name

Date

First House (self)

Second House (money)

Third House (movement)

Fourth House (home)

Fifth House (love)

Sixth House (work)

Seventh House (partners)

Eighth House (changes)

Ninth House (self-development)

Tenth House (life-path)

Eleventh House (results)

Twelfth House (hidden issues)

Center

Notice to print shops:
The owner of this book has permission to make copies of this blank spread form for personal use only.

These forms are not for resale, nor are they to be scanned or shared on the internet in any form.

Elizabeth Hazel © 2020 Kozmic Kitchen Press
For more information or use for educational purposes contact Liz at
www.kozmickitchenpress.com

THE SPIRAL 12-HOUSE SPREAD — VARIATION 2

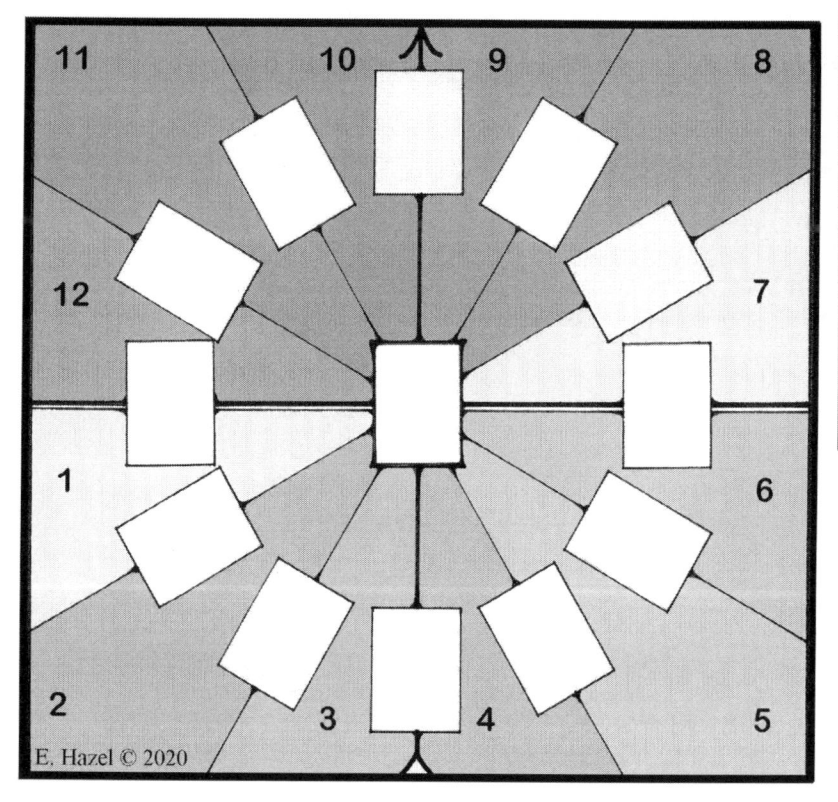

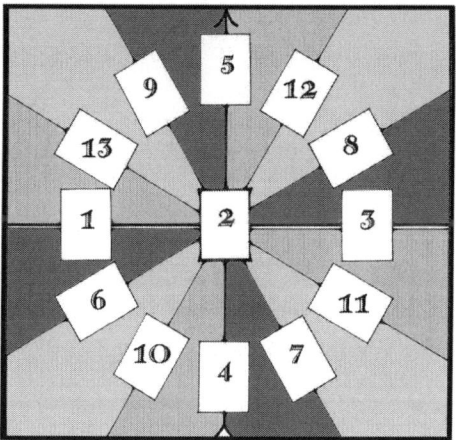

Name

Date

First House (self)

Second House (money)

Third House (movement)

Fourth House (home)

Fifth House (love)

Sixth House (work)

Seventh House (partners)

Eighth House (changes)

Ninth House (self-development)

Tenth House (life-path)

Eleventh House (results)

Twelfth House (hidden issues)

Center

Notice to print shops:
The owner of this book has permission to make copies of this blank spread form for personal use only.

These forms are not for resale, nor are they to be scanned or shared on the internet in any form.

Elizabeth Hazel © 2020 Kozmic Kitchen Press
For more information or use for educational purposes contact Liz at
www.kozmickitchenpress.com

THE SPIRAL 12-HOUSE SPREAD — VARIATION 3 EXPANDED

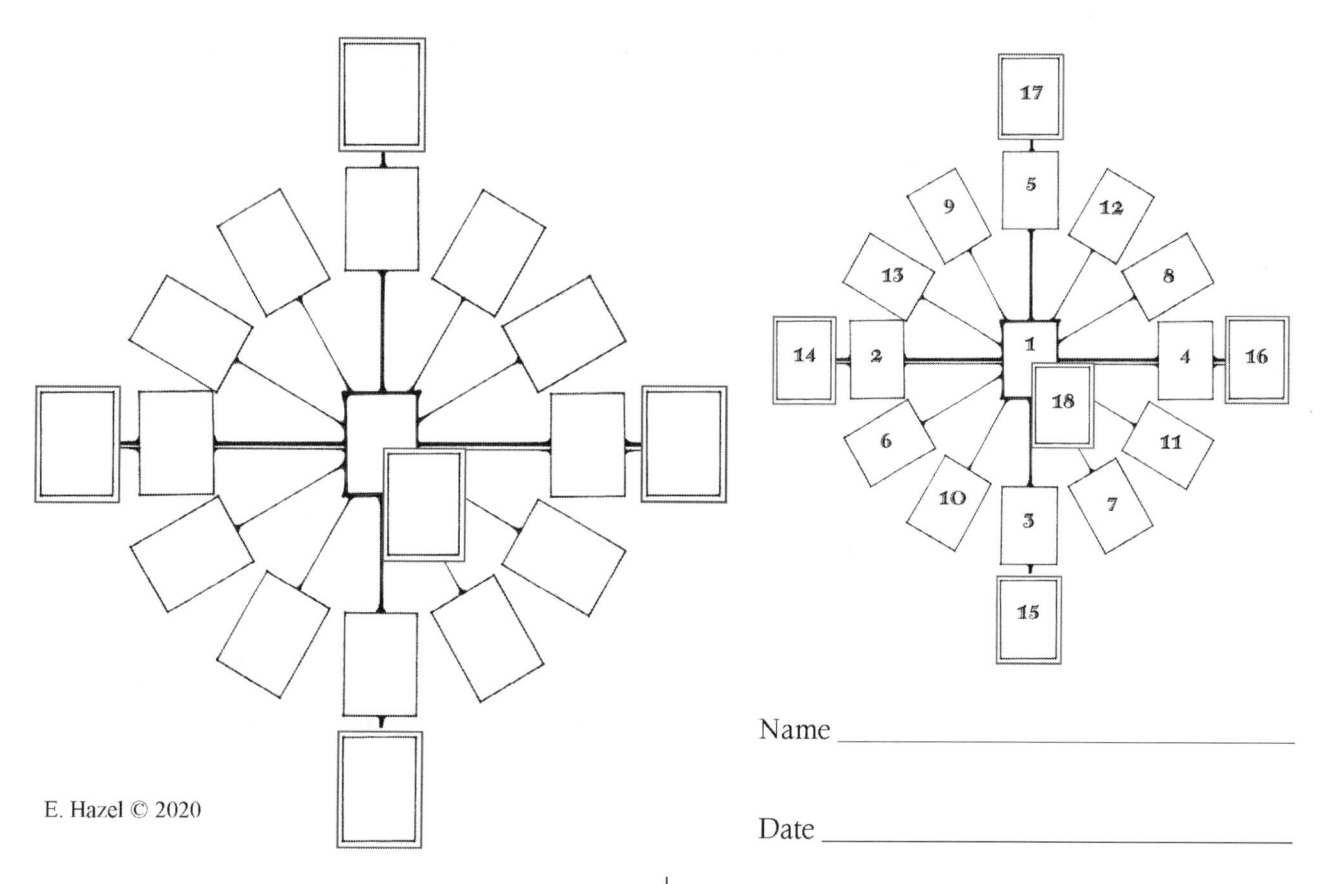

E. Hazel © 2020

Name _____

Date _____

Center

First House (self)

Second House (money)

Third House (movement)

Fourth House (home)

Fifth House (love)

Sixth House (work)

Seventh House (partners)

Eighth House (changes)

Ninth House (self-development)

Tenth House (life-path)

Eleventh House (results)

Twelfth House (hidden issues)

Ascendant Cover Card

IC Cover Card

Descendant Cover Card

MC Cover Card

Central Cover Card

Notice to print shops:
The owner of this book has permission to make copies of this blank spread form for personal use only.

These forms are not for resale, nor are they to be scanned or shared on the internet in any form.

Elizabeth Hazel © 2020 Kozmic Kitchen Press
For more information or use for educational purposes contact Liz at
www.kozmickitchenpress.com

THE VALA CROSS SPREAD

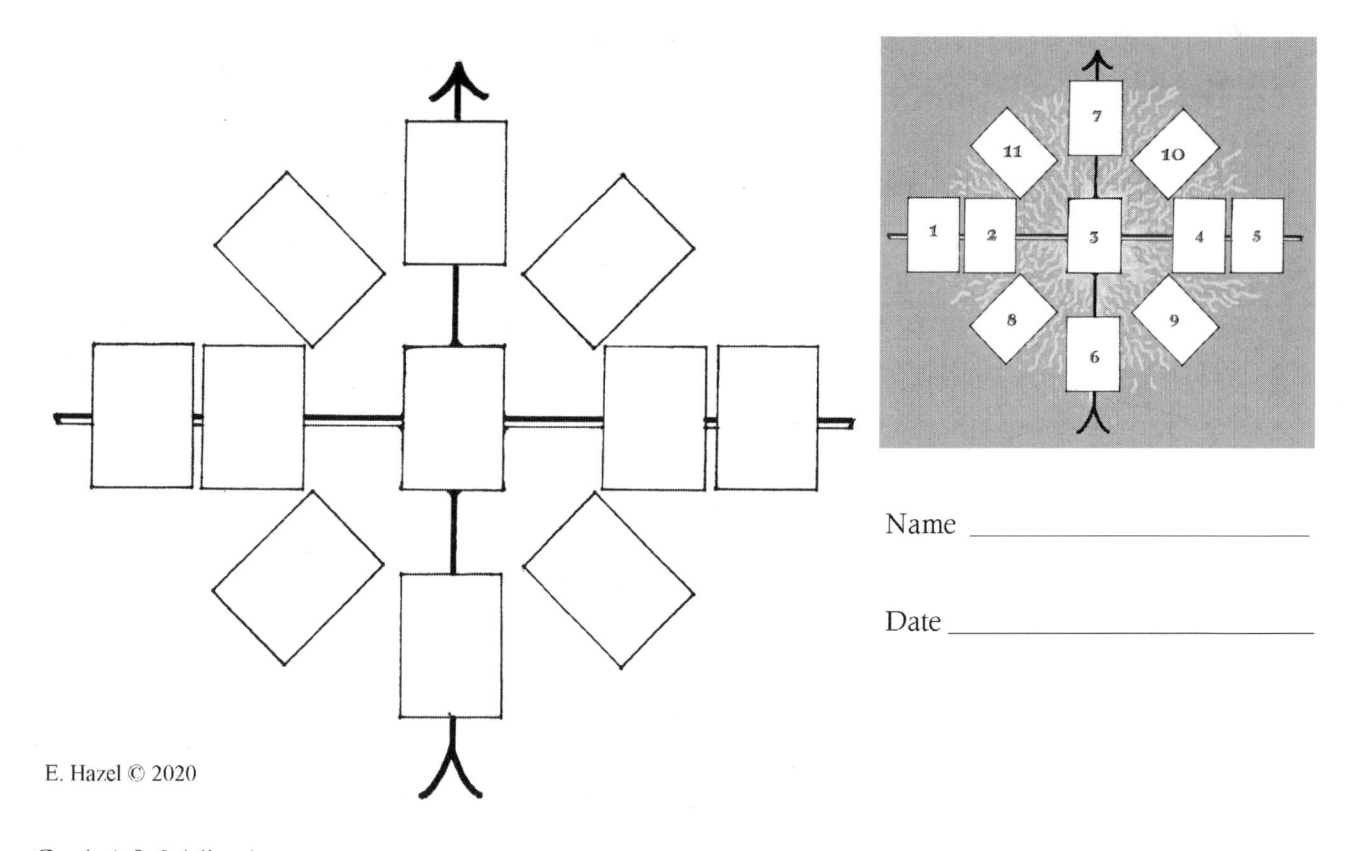

E. Hazel © 2020

Name _____

Date _____

Cards 1 & 2 (client)

Card 3 (current)

Cards 4 & 5 (others)

Card 6 (inner life)

Card 7 (outer life, future)

Card 8 (personal assets)

Card 9 (relationships)

Card 10 (transitions)

Card 11 (results)

Notice to print shops:
The owner of this book has permission to make copies of this blank spread form for personal use only.

These forms are not for resale, nor are they to be scanned or shared on the internet in any form.

Elizabeth Hazel © 2020 Kozmic Kitchen Press
For more information or use for educational purposes contact Liz at
www.kozmickitchenpress.com

THE EXPANDED VALA CROSS SPREAD

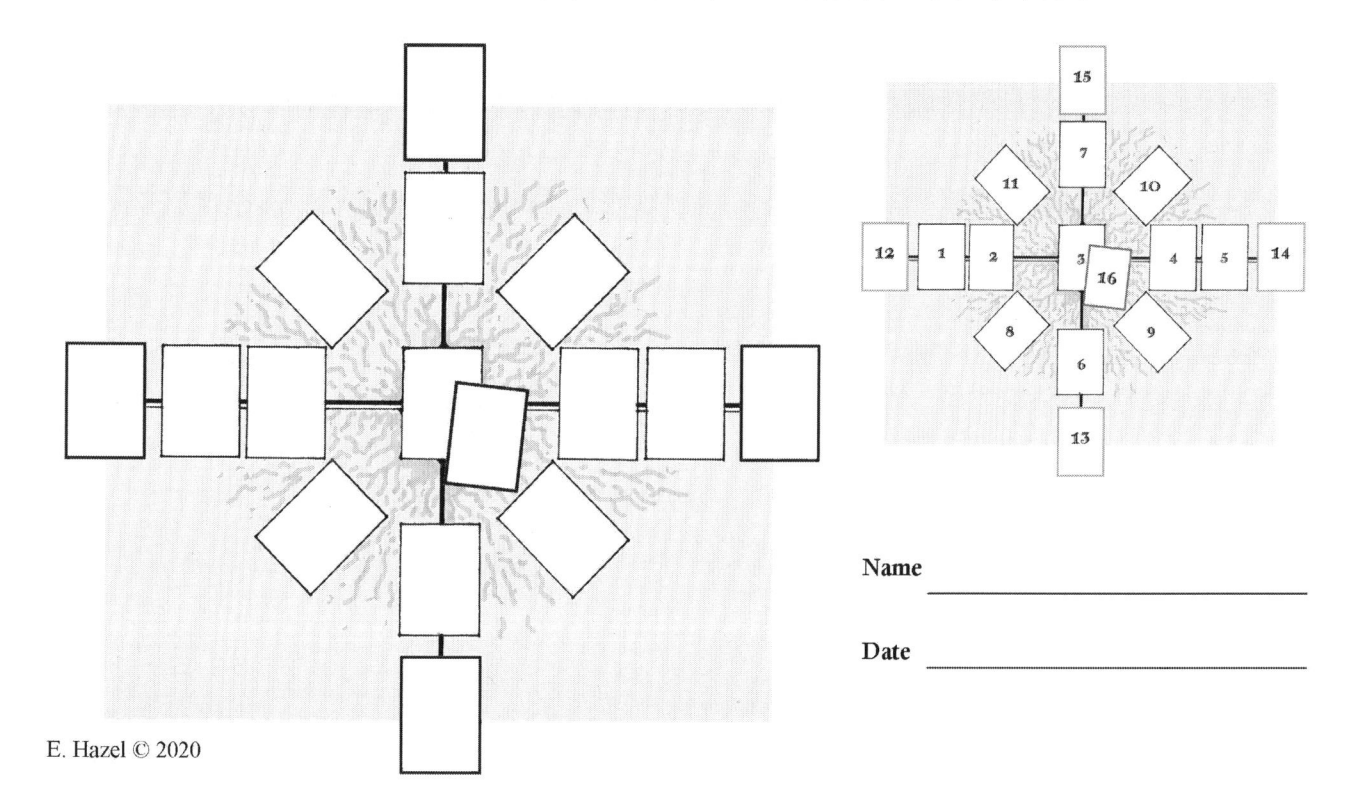

E. Hazel © 2020

Name _____

Date _____

Cards 1 & 2 (client)

Card 3 (current)

Cards 4 & 5 (others)

Card 6 (inner life)

Card 7 (outer life, future)

Card 8 (personal assets)

Card 9 (relationships)

Card 10 (transitions)

Card 11 (results)

Cover Card 12 (client)

Cover Card 13 (inner life)

Cover Card 14 (others)

Cover Card 15 (life-path)

Center Cover Card 16 (summary)

Notice to print shops:
The owner of this book has permission to make copies of this blank spread form for personal use only.

These forms are not for resale, nor are they to be scanned or shared on the internet in any form.

Elizabeth Hazel © 2020 Kozmic Kitchen Press
For more information or use for educational purposes contact Liz at
www.kozmickitchenpress.com

THE EXPANDED COSMIC CROSS SPREAD – VARIATION 1

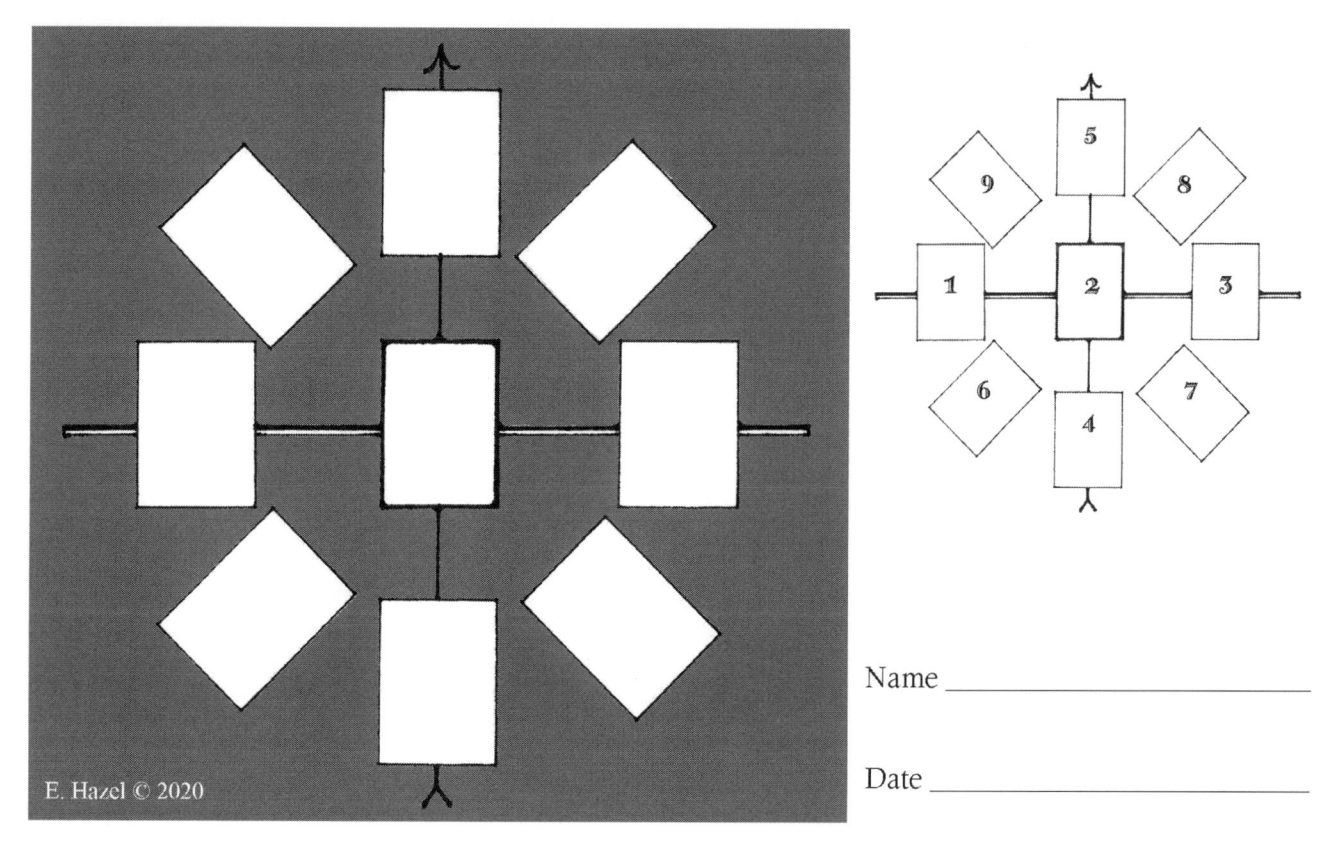

Name _____

Date _____

Card 1 (self)

Card 2 (current)

Card 3 (others)

Card 4 (inner life)

Card 5 (life-path)

Card 6 (personal assets)

Card 7 (relationships)

Card 8 (transitions)

Card 9 (results)

Twelve-House Tarot Spreads

Notice to print shops:
The owner of this book has permission to make copies of this blank spread form for personal use only.

These forms are not for resale, nor are they to be scanned or shared on the internet in any form.

Elizabeth Hazel © 2020 Kozmic Kitchen Press
For more information or use for educational purposes contact Liz at
www.kozmickitchenpress.com

THE EXPANDED COSMIC CROSS SPREAD – VARIATION 2

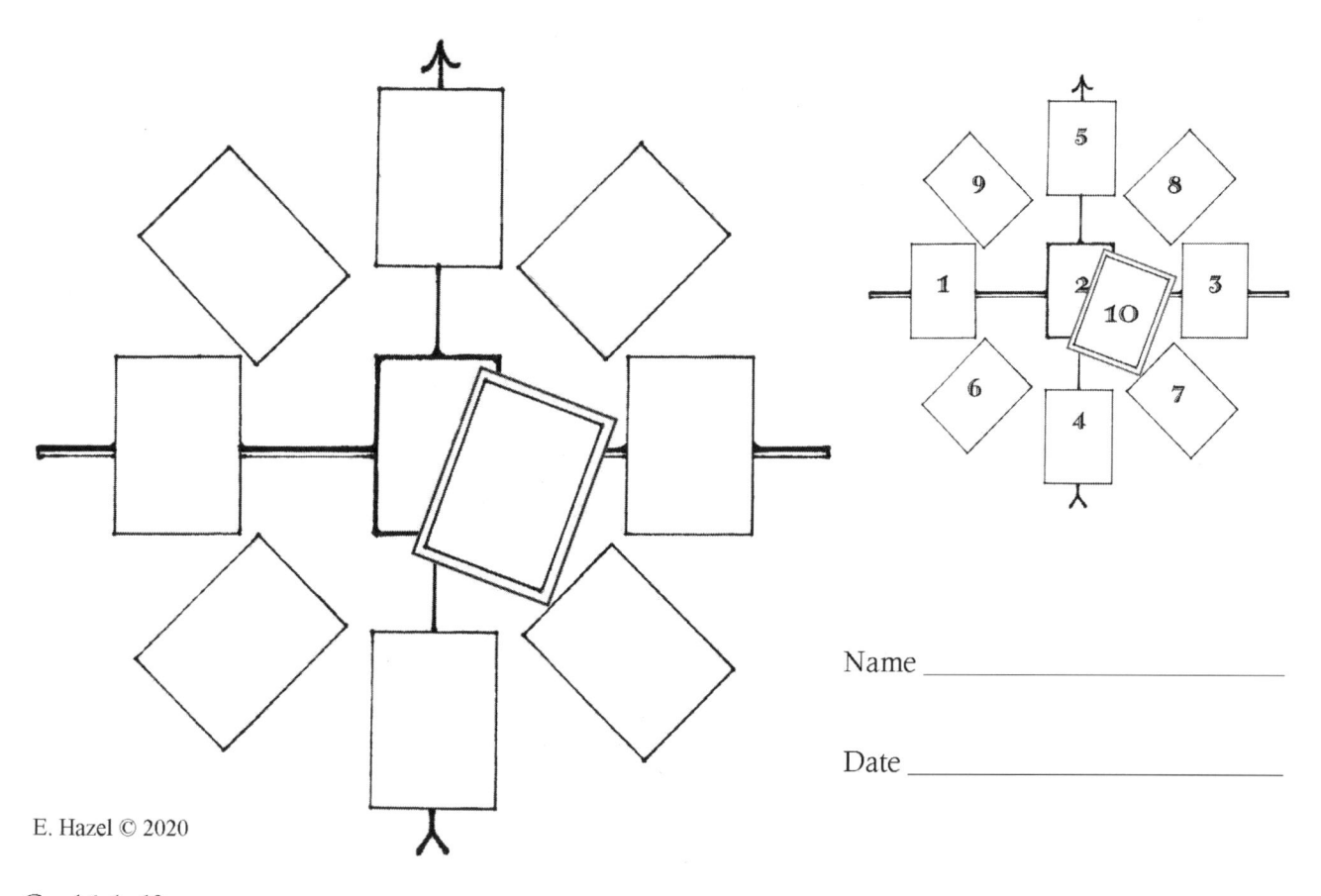

Name _____

Date _____

E. Hazel © 2020

Card 1 (self)

Card 2 (current)

Card 3 (others)

Card 4 (inner life)

Card 5 (life-path)

Card 6 (personal assets)

Card 7 (relationships)

Card 8 (transitions)

Card 9 (results)

Cover Card 10 (summary)

Notice to print shops:
The owner of this book has permission to make copies of this blank spread form for personal use only.

These forms are not for resale, nor are they to be scanned or shared on the internet in any form.

Elizabeth Hazel © 2020 Kozmic Kitchen Press
For more information or use for educational purposes contact Liz at
www.kozmickitchenpress.com

Twelve-House Tarot Spreads   Appendix —Blank Spread Forms   109

THE EXPANDED COSMIC CROSS SPREAD – VARIATION 3

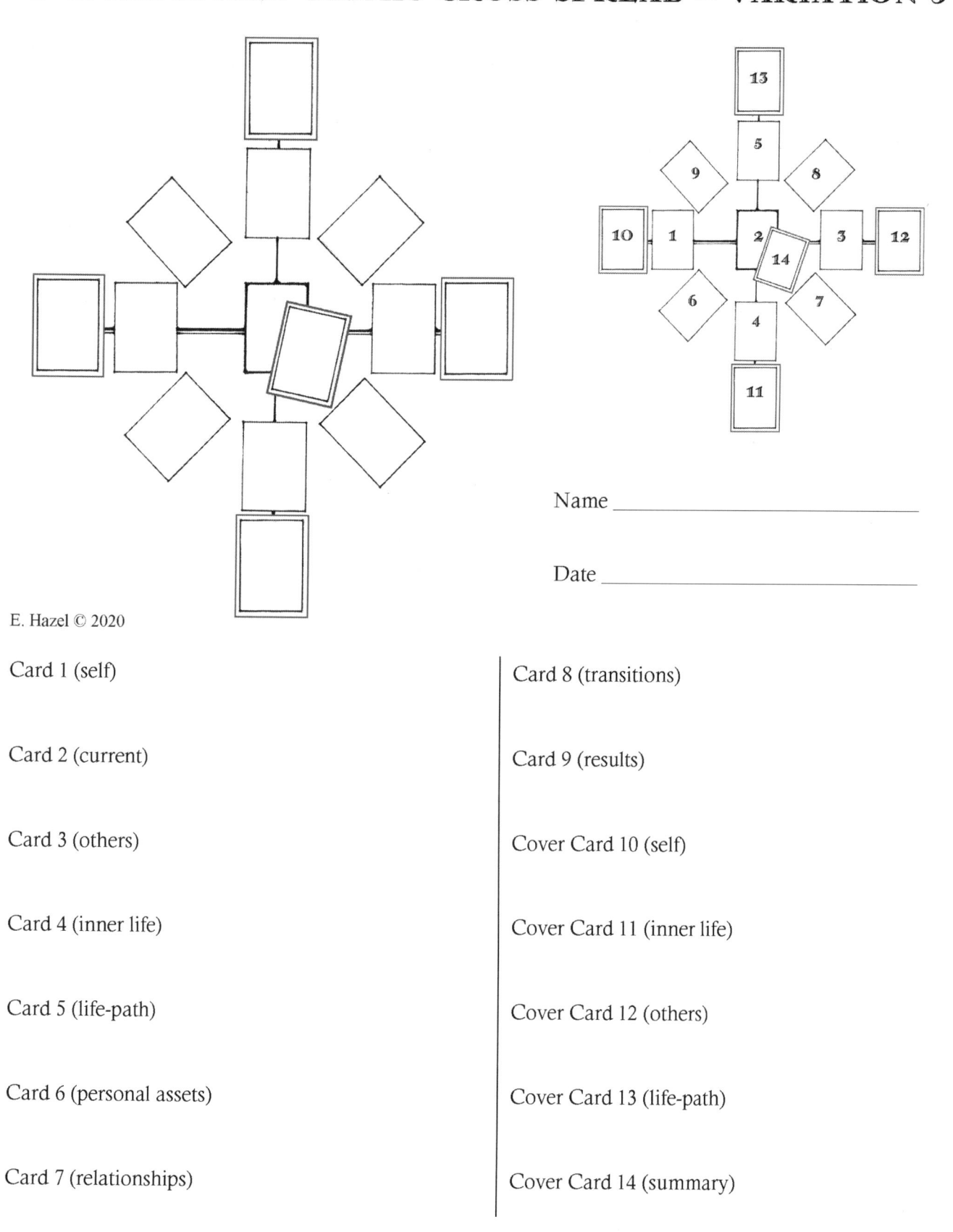

E. Hazel © 2020

Name _____

Date _____

Card 1 (self)

Card 2 (current)

Card 3 (others)

Card 4 (inner life)

Card 5 (life-path)

Card 6 (personal assets)

Card 7 (relationships)

Card 8 (transitions)

Card 9 (results)

Cover Card 10 (self)

Cover Card 11 (inner life)

Cover Card 12 (others)

Cover Card 13 (life-path)

Cover Card 14 (summary)

Notice to print shops:
The owner of this book has permission to make copies of this blank spread form for personal use only.

These forms are not for resale, nor are they to be scanned or shared on the internet in any form.

Elizabeth Hazel © 2020 Kozmic Kitchen Press
For more information or use for educational purposes contact Liz at
www.kozmickitchenpress.com

THE EIGHT-FOLD PATH SABBAT SPREAD

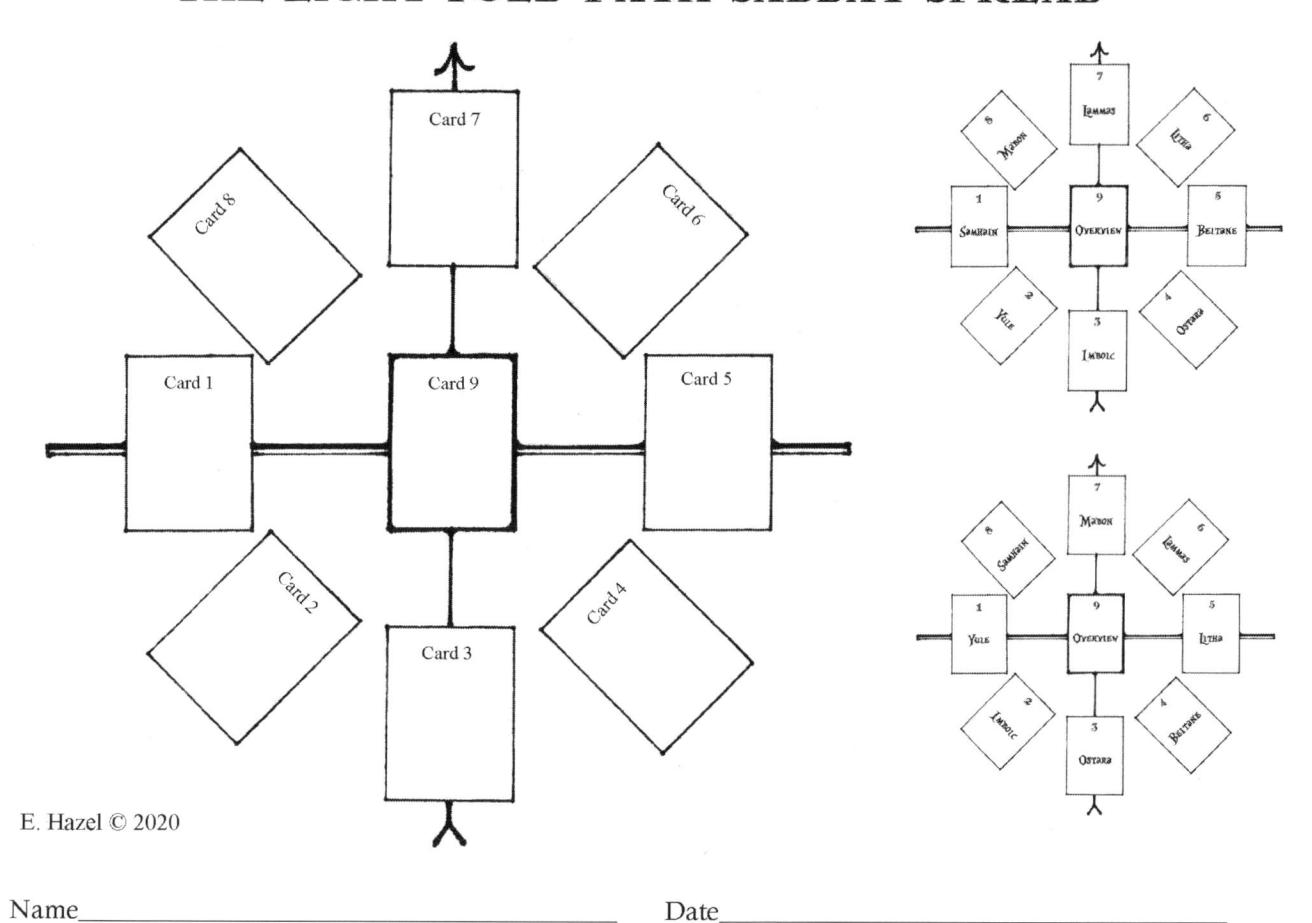

Name_____ Date_____

(indicate the sabbat of each card)

Card 1

Card 2

Card 3

Card 4

Card 5

Card 6

Card 7

Card 8

Card 9 (summary)

Notice to print shops:
The owner of this book has permission to make copies of this blank spread form for personal use only.

These forms are not for resale, nor are they to be scanned or shared on the internet in any form.

Elizabeth Hazel © 2020 Kozmic Kitchen Press
For more information or use for educational purposes contact Liz at
www.kozmickitchenpress.com

THE ETTEILLA 12-HOUSE HORARY SPREAD

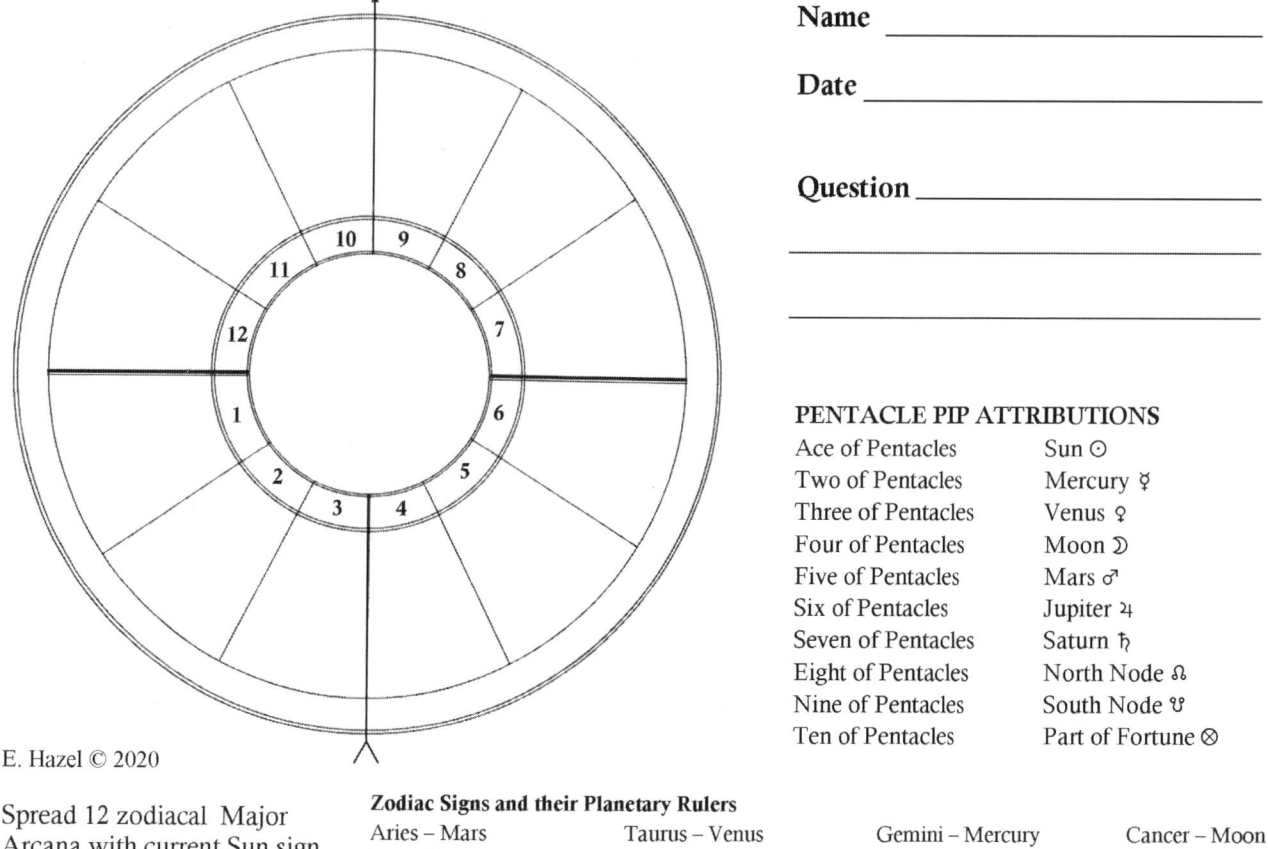

Name _____

Date _____

Question _____
_____
_____

PENTACLE PIP ATTRIBUTIONS

Ace of Pentacles	Sun ☉
Two of Pentacles	Mercury ☿
Three of Pentacles	Venus ♀
Four of Pentacles	Moon ☽
Five of Pentacles	Mars ♂
Six of Pentacles	Jupiter ♃
Seven of Pentacles	Saturn ♄
Eight of Pentacles	North Node ☊
Nine of Pentacles	South Node ☋
Ten of Pentacles	Part of Fortune ⊗

E. Hazel © 2020

Spread 12 zodiacal Major Arcana with current Sun sign in the first house.

Zodiac Signs and their Planetary Rulers

Aries – Mars	Taurus – Venus	Gemini – Mercury	Cancer – Moon
Leo – Sun	Virgo – Mercury	Libra – Venus	Scorpio – Mars
Sagittarius – Jupiter	Capricorn – Saturn	Aquarius – Saturn	Pisces – Jupiter

Planetary Significators

Querent—Planetary significator (ruler of first house sun-sign) and the Moon

    House & sign of planet

    House & sign of Moon

Quesited—Planetary significator of object, personal, or goal of question

    Ruled by which house?

    House and sign where significator is located

Is there an aspect relationship between the querent's and quesited's significators?

Quick Answer Tips: If both planets are in even-numbered houses, or both in odd-numbered houses, the answer will probably be "yes." If one significator planet is in an even-numbered house, and the other is in an odd-numbered house, the answer is probably "no." The answer is more definitively *yes* or *no* if one of the significator planets is in a pivotal house (1st – 4th – 7th – 10th). If the querent's significator makes no aspect to the quesited's significator, compare the position of the Moon to the significator of the quesited with the same criteria.

Notice to print shops:
The owner of this book has permission to make copies of this blank spread form for personal use only.

These forms are not for resale, nor are they to be scanned or shared on the internet in any form.

Elizabeth Hazel © 2020 Kozmic Kitchen Press
For more information or use for educational purposes contact Liz at
www.kozmickitchenpress.com

ABOUT THE AUTHOR

Elizabeth Hazel is an astrologer, tarotist, author and speaker. She has studied tarot since age 11, and in case you're curious, her first tarot deck was *The Aquarian Tarot* by David Palladini. She realized this deck, although beautiful, left something to be desired and returned to the shop to purchase the *Harris-Crowley Thoth Tarot* three weeks later. The glyphs included on the cards spurred her to study astrology. Liz studied alone, reading every book she could find until she graduated from college (Bachelor's of Music Composition and Theory, Miami University, Oxford, Ohio). College friends bugged her to give them readings, and it doesn't take a genius to figure out what happened after that. She studied astrology with Dr. Rilma Buckman from 1983 to 1986 and started participating in local psychic fairs. She also made several trips to Italy and acquired a number of unusual tarot decks.

Liz became conversant with Jungian Depth Astrology and applying myths to chart interpretations. She became interested in Vedic (Jyotish/Hindu) astrology in the early 1990s and jumped from that to ancient Hellenic astrology when books by Project Hindsight were published in the mid-1990s. Around the same time she started writing articles for the *International Tarot Association Journal* (a peer-reviewed publication).

Her first published work was **Tarot Decoded: Using and Understanding Dignities and Attributions** (Weiser, 2004). She spent several years creating the art work for her original tarot deck, **The Whispering Tarot deck and book** (2008). Liz was active with the American Tarot Association for several years and became the editor of the *American Tarot Association Quarterly Journal* in 2006. She established her own imprint, Kozmic Kitchen Press, in 2008, and has recently published **Little Book of Fixed Stars: Expanded Second Edition** with contributing author Michael Munkasey and **Antiscia: Secrets in the Mirror** (2020).

She joined NCGR's SMARRT (Ann Arbor) chapter and became a board member in 2010. She is a frequent contributor to NCGR's *ENews*, *Quarterly Memberletter*, and *Geocosmic Journal*, and has been published in the *ISAR Journal* and *The Mountain Astrologer*, along with other magazines and newspapers.

Liz has given presentations on tarot, astrology, and metaphysical topics around the US and Great Britain. She is a regular presenter at the Great Lakes Astrology Conference and presented *Antiscia: Secrets in the Mirror* at UAC 2018 in Chicago. She continues to write, lecture, and organize regional astrology events.

Liz lives in Toledo, Ohio, with her spoiled kitties and a ridiculously large number of tarot decks and books. She offers this tip for other people in a similar situation, "If you have to move, pack your books and tarot decks in tote bags. They're easier to carry than boxes."

If you enjoyed this book, check out **Tarot Decoded** (2004) and the new follow-up book **Attributions in Naked Splendor**, available in late September 2020.

BOOKS BY ELIZABETH HAZEL

Little Book of Fixed Stars: Expanded Second Edition (May 2020)
Antiscia: Secrets in the Mirror (August 2020)
The Advanced Tarot-Astrology Series:
Twelve-House Tarot Spread: Uses and Variations (September 2020)
Attributions in Naked Splendor (late September 2020)

The Whispering Tarot signed limited edition of 900 copies, 2008 ($25) and
The Whispering Tarot: Softly Spoken Secrets book ($16)

Tarot Decoded: Understanding and Using Correspondences and Dignities (Red Wheel/Weiser, 2004) paperback and e-book

✳✳✳

PRIVATE PRINTINGS
Little Book of Fixed Stars, first edition 2017 ($15)
Geomantic Divination, 2013 ($10)
Lady Vala's Little Book of Mantras, 3rd edition 2014 ($9)
Lady Vala's Little Book of Sabbats, 3rd edition 2014 ($10.50)
(contact the author for purchase, some titles have limited availability)

COMING SOON FROM KOZMIC KITCHEN PRESS

Astrological texts:
Metaphysical Cosmos
The Evolution of Chiron
Lady Asteroids Vesta and Ceres: A New Perspective
Lady Asteroids Pallas Athena and Juno: A New Perspective

KOZMIC KITCHEN PRESS

www.kozmickitchenpress.com